LEVEL UP

HOW LEADERS DO LESS AND BE MORE

Grammar Factory Publishing
MacMillan Company Limited
25 Telegram Mews, 39th Floor, Suite 3906
Toronto, Ontario, Canada
M5V 3Z1

www.grammarfactory.com

Burgess, Maree, 1961–
Level Up: How Leaders Do Less and Be More / Maree Burgess.

Paperback ISBN 978-1-989737-46-0
Hardcover ISBN 978-1-989737-48-4
eBook ISBN 978-1-989737-47-7

    1. BUS059000 BUSINESS & ECONOMICS / Skills. 2. BUS071000 BUSINESS & ECONOMICS / Leadership. 3. BUS041000 BUSINESS & ECONOMICS / Management.

Production Credits
Cover design by Designerbility
Interior layout design by Dania Zafar
Book production and editorial services by Grammar Factory Publishing

Grammar Factory's Carbon Neutral Publishing Commitment
From January 1st, 2020 onwards, Grammar Factory Publishing is proud to be neutralizing the carbon footprint of all printed copies of its authors' books printed by or ordered directly through Grammar Factory or its affiliated companies through the purchase of Gold Standard-Certified International Offsets.

Disclaimer
The material in this publication is of the nature of general comment only and does not represent professional advice. It is not intended to provide specific guidance for particular circumstances, and it should not be relied on as the basis for any decision to take action or not take action on any matter which it covers. Readers should obtain professional advice where appropriate, before making any such decision. To the maximum extent permitted by law, the author and publisher disclaim all responsibility and liability to any person, arising directly or indirectly from any person taking or not taking action based on the information in this publication.

LEVEL UP

HOW LEADERS DO LESS AND BE MORE

MAREE BURGESS

Testimonials

'Maree has addressed what can be a challenging time in a new leader's life by providing them with a handbook for success. Every chapter is filled with practical tools, checklists, and activities to help them level up from being a contributor to a manager and leader. A must-read for any new manager who is stepping up from their technical excellence and wants to develop leadership excellence.'

Donna McGeorge

Best-selling author of *The 25-Minute Meeting: Half the Time, Double the Impact* and *The First 2 Hours: Make Better Use of Your Most Valuable Time*

'This book is simply brilliant. There is nothing more ineffective and exhausting than trying to do a whole team's job, and nothing more frustrating than working for someone who does your job. It's hard to let go, but you will be amazed what happens once you do. The strategies and tips in this book will literally change your life and give you time back. Maree is a genius at outlining step by step how to make this liberating transition. Level Up is a must-read for new leaders, not-so-new leaders who need a reminder, or for those who are struggling with an endless cycle of busyness!'

Simone Van Veen
Chief Member Officer, Bank First

'A great book for every leader who is moving up a level and needs to stop doing the work of their team. Full of practical advice and checklists, immediately actionable.'

Carolyn Taylor

Author of *Walking the Talk: Building a Culture for Success*

'Level Up *fills a gap in the business literature. Transitioning from management to leadership is a continuous effort in which many great professionals often get lost. Unlike many theory-heavy books,* Level Up *provided me with a great mix of practical advice, tutorial-like approaches, tasks, and thought-provoking perspectives that can guide you through this challenging phase of your career. Some of the key messages around embracing delegation as a way to become a better leader but also to empower your teams are truly game-changers. I'll be thinking about asking the right questions as opposed to having all the answers from now on. Thank you, Maree!'*

Anthony Pagès

Chief Executive Officer, ANU Enterprise Pty. Ltd.

'Insightful and practical, this book by Maree Burgess is a treasure trove for new leaders who want to create the best habits and thinking for the leadership journey. The checklists, reflection tools, and strategies are gold for people who know that the key to getting better at the profession of leading is to first build self-awareness. This is some of the best advice I have ever read on how to level up.'

Tracey Ezard

Author, speaker, and creator of Ferocious Warmth Leadership

'Evolving as a leader is possible – and necessary – and yet quite often, people don't know how to do so, either practically or emotionally. In this book, Maree Burgess uses her experiences, observations, and understanding of the dynamics of managing and leading to help both new and veteran leaders level up in their roles.

'This is not just a philosophy with no practical applications: it's a step-by-step model of behavioural and mindset change that can be implemented, replicated, and modelled. Maree's book exposes the consequences of older, ineffective ways of thinking about leadership and guides readers towards more efficient alternatives. It's a must-read for all managers and leaders who have too much on, too much to do, or aren't making the progress they would like. Bravo!'

Lynne Cazaly
Speaker and author of *Better Ways of Thinking & Working: How Changing the Way You Do Things, Changes What You Can Do* and *Argh! Too Much Information, Not Enough Brain: A Practical Guide to Outsmarting Overwhelm*

'Maree has provided much-needed perspective to my role as a leader. I highly value her experience and positivity in helping me negotiate a balance amongst multiple demands to achieve my professional goals. Level Up explores concepts that are vital to becoming a sustainable leader in any field.'

Katrina
Medical practitioner

'Insightful and instructive, this book is a must-read for anyone wanting to level up their leadership skills and unleash the brilliance within. Packed full of helpful exercises and examples, this beautifully written book will help you become a better leader of yourself and others.'

Janine Garner
Best-selling author of Be Brilliant: How to Lead a Life of Influence **and** It's Who You Know: How to Make Networking Work for You

Contents

About Maree

Maree supports leaders and teams to create cultures that people want to be part of and perform at their best for. For the past thirty years, she has worked with numerous leaders, teams and organisations (including NAB, Red Cross Lifeblood, L'Oréal, the Department of Education and Monash University) all over Australia, helping them communicate more effectively to get the results they are looking for.

Maree knows that there can be occasional challenges in working with and managing people, and she draws upon a vast skillset developed throughout her career to show her clients how to build engagement, elevate performance, and move through change. Having begun her career as a registered nurse at a major Melbourne trauma hospital, followed by several senior roles in banking and over seventeen years as an expert behavioural consultant, she is equipped with the resolve and knowledge to connect and inspire any mix of people.

Armed with a deep understanding of workplace behaviour, Maree has trained in models of excellence to a high level. She is a Graduate in Neuro-Behavioural Modelling, Certified in C-IQ

(Conversational Intelligence), a trainer and master practitioner of NLP (Neuro Linguistic Programming), a certified mBIT coach (multiple Brain Integration Technique), an accredited administer of GENOS instruments (Emotional Intelligence), and an administrator of MBTI (Myers-Briggs Type Indicator).

Maree is an expert at facilitating workshops, providing leadership and communication skills training, coaching middle and senior management, and providing support to senior leaders across a range of industries. Her expertise helps individuals and teams build focus, perspective, and behavioural and conversational agility. She is known for getting people to lift their performance, operate at the right level, and lift their team to become more effective.

Maree obsesses about potential because in her very first role – a position in a forestry commission in rural New South Wales, which she got when she was a teenager – she lucked into having a boss who empowered her and let her explore and discover what she could do well. She was allowed to revamp several systems within the office, from how to manage bee-leasing sites to tracking logging in public forests. Those nine months set her up for how she has spent the rest of her career – enjoying herself.

Contrast that with a later role in a major bank, where every day (pretty much) she would catch a lift to her floor with a colleague who said *every single time* 'another day, another dollar' and, as the lift door opened, finished by saying 'less tax'.This was a person who wasn't passionate and didn't enjoy much about their role, or their boss, or the wider organisation. They were there for the pay cheque and not much else.

Maree became curious about this lack of engagement as she started to explore what made people happy, and even passionate, about their work. She couldn't understand why people who spent more time at work than anywhere else didn't find ways to enjoy what they did. The coaching business that Maree started in 2003 (which now includes training, facilitating, speaking and writing) focuses on locating people's strengths and making them tap into their potential, allowing them to find greater happiness in their work.

When she's not writing, coaching, or standing at the front of the room training leaders and teams (or in front of a computer using Zoom!), Maree enjoys walking with her husband and two dogs along the beach close to her home, curling up on a couch reading a ~~trashy novel~~ business book, or hanging out in the Strathbogie Ranges eating slow-cooked food and drinking red wine!

INTRODUCTION

It's early on Monday morning. You've spent the weekend trying to catch up on the work you didn't get done last week. There is so much to do, and your team has dropped the ball – again.

Sending work back to redo is making them resentful. Redoing it yourself is making *you* resentful. Let's face it, it would have been easier to do it yourself in the first place.

There is a queue of people at your desk, or sending you instant messages, or asking you questions. It's faster to give the answer than take the time to help them work it out for themselves.

You're going to more meetings, including those with members of your team, because you want to stay across everything and make sure the team is getting it right. You're starting work earlier, finishing later, then working again after the family is in bed. And don't even mention finding time for regular exercise, sleep or eating well.

Your boss wants you to start focusing on future goals and addressing current results, but there is no time for that yet.

You wanted this role because you love what you do, and you know deep down that you can do a good job. What you hadn't considered is that all your relationships with the team have changed - you are *managing* the team when you used to be *part* of the team.

It feels like your team members are holding back, and the camaraderie you used to enjoy has disappeared. Some individuals in the team are behaving differently and proving difficult to manage. Bad behaviour is prevalent, and the team culture isn't what it used to be.

It's not your fault that you're stuck in a vicious cycle of reacting, redoing and responding – something that is typical of those in a middle-management role. Quite simply, this is because:

Mid-level managers, and new managers, are not taught to lead.

You are now leading a team, but you only know how to manage one – you are doing the transactional stuff.

But it's been assumed by the people around you that you know how to lead because you were so good at what you did in previous roles. You are in this role or have recently been promoted into it because you are very good at the technical skills; however, these rarely translate into great leadership skills.

You continue doing the work you used to do. This is your comfort zone – you know what to do, and you are very good at it. But this means you are neglecting your team and not focusing on the work required at this level of seniority. The people stuff is piling up, and you are drowning in busyness.

Who you were in your old job, is not what is required in this job.

In his book *What Got You Here Won't Get You There: How Successful People Become Even More Successful*, Marshall Goldsmith shares the importance of developing or changing behavioural skills rather than technical skills as you move into more senior roles.

Technical skills are the skills that have got you to where you are. These skills are what you need to perform specific tasks. Sometimes called 'hard' skills, they are the abilities and knowledge you have acquired in your area of expertise. Examples of technical skills are things like programming, project management, or managing a balance sheet.

In management roles these technical skills are not required to the same extent, because there is a team in place to do this work. Behavioural skills, also called 'soft' or 'people' skills, are needed as you start to lead people. Behavioural skills include things like communication and listening, being able to deal with challenging people, giving and receiving feedback, building rapport, delegating, and managing conflict.

Over the past twenty years, I've had the honour of working with hundreds of leaders across a range of industries – from large corporates, to small- to medium-size companies, to those in the not-for-profit sector. I have consistently found that the middle layer of an organisation is where culture emerges. Yet this layer is the most under-supported in terms of leadership and behavioural skill development. This is where overwhelm is rife.

I love working with mid-level leaders and their teams. Without a doubt, they want to improve, learn how to lead effectively, and build teams that want to be better engaged and do good work together. And you can do that, too – all it takes is a mindset shift and some improvement in your behavioural skills.

Then, you can start focusing on:

- Doing less of the work that your team should be doing, and
- Building your team's capability so they can perform better and take on more responsibility.

This is why this book focuses on key behavioural skills that shift you from being a Transactional Manager to a Transformational Leader.

The skills I share in this book are the basics that underpin leadership development, and will allow you to move on to bigger and better things.

So, are you ready to step into your role and lead at the level you need to achieve success?

HOW TO USE THIS BOOK

This book is light on theory and heavy on practicality, with lots of exercises and questionnaires. I use a little bit of neuroscience and Neuro Linguistic Programming to explain the changes you want to make.

Everything I cover here mimics what I regularly share in my workshops, leadership programs, and one-on-one leadership coaching sessions. It is all road-tested with real people who struggled with the same issues you are struggling with now.

What you will read is practical and easy to implement.

There are activities in each chapter, so have some highlighters, colourful pens and Post-it Notes handy.

Write on the pages any notes, thoughts or 'aha' moments you may be experiencing. Highlight sections and complete the questionnaires, even if you only do so in your head!

I love to see a good, dog-eared book with lots of notes throughout.

If you're someone who hates to tag or write in a book, go over to my website, www.mareeburgess.com/levelup, to download an editable online workbook, which includes all the activities in this book, plus a few special bonuses.

My wish for you is to identify the areas you want to work on and implement the changes you need to become a better leader. Ultimately, this will help you do less and be more.

One thing you can do to achieve this is to take action, big or small.

I've divided this book in two parts to guide your success.

Part I is about identifying where you are now on your leadership journey, and what issues you are likely to experience.

Part II is about giving you the tools and exercises you need to help you lead at the right level. This is the practical part of the book, and is packed with tools and techniques to help you tap into both your own brilliance, and the brilliance of your team.

PART ONE

WHY LEVEL UP

When you step into a management role, you often act by default.

It is assumed that when people move from a 'doing' role to a 'managing' role, they will know what they need to do. Little thought is given to training or supporting these managers to learn to lead.

There is less budget for lifting the management skills of mid-level leaders than for leaders in more senior roles.

Mid-level managers are often accused of being control freaks or micromanagers by their staff. There is so much to do, and it is often quicker and easier to do it yourself than ask your team to do it.

This leads to overwhelm and exhaustion. Which leads to even more micromanagement or controlling behaviour.

It is a known fact that while people may join an organisation for specific reasons, they leave because of their manager. And usually, it's because that manager has been too controlling.

This is wrong-level leadership, which means the manager is operating at a level (or two) below where they should be. This is ineffective and pushes the team down, so they are also operating at a lower level.

Don't let this be you.

This book will help you learn how to identify if you are at the ineffective end of the scale in terms of leadership, or at the transformational end.

CHAPTER 1:

ADMIT IT, YOU'RE A BIT OF A CONTROL FREAK

Amy can pinpoint the moment she realised she was operating at the wrong level.

Up to that moment, she thought she was doing okay in her new leadership role. When she stepped into this position, her first time leading a team, she was beyond excited. She knew the team – heck, she'd been part of them. And now, she was their leader.

She continued working as she had previously. She focused on her work – which was pretty much the same as what she had been doing in her old role – and expected the team to focus on theirs.

Amy had been exceptional in her old role. She was a technical expert and a star performer for the team. That's why, when her boss moved on, she was promoted into his role.

Her style initially was very hands-off. She had previously been a siloed operator, and assumed everyone else behaved the same way by taking responsibility for completing what they needed to do.

———————————

*Amy was slow to realise that the skills that
had got her to this spot were not the ones
she needed to lead her current team.*

———————————

All the things she was doing in that initial year almost set her up for failure. The team was becoming alienated – not just from Amy, but from each other.

A few key players in the team started to actively conspire against Amy. Her boss was trying to be supportive, but started to wonder whether she really was the right person for the role.

The moment Amy realised she was operating at the wrong level was when she got the results from the organisation-wide engagement survey, and the comments made by her team about her leadership style were damning.

This led to her HR (human resources) business partner mediating between her and two members of her team. The feedback from those team members was terrible, and Amy's confidence took a complete battering.

They accused her of micromanaging and almost standing over them to do their work. They said that Amy criticised anything they did, and often took work back from them and redid it. As deadlines loomed, she took more and more work off the team, as she didn't believe they were doing it the 'right' way.

Amy was so anxious to succeed that she was acting autonomously and not engaging her team. She was working longer and longer hours, and becoming frustrated with what her team weren't doing.

I met Amy about six months after this intervention, and she was still feeling bruised. She was also confused about what she was expected to do as a leader.

---

*Leading a team is quite different
from being part of that team.*

WHAT LEVEL ARE YOU LEADING AT?

Of course, leading at the wrong level doesn't only apply to managers in the middle of an organisation, it applies across the board.

A CEO once told me how they were struggling with their team. They had a group of executives who were too immersed in the details of day-to-day operations, and it was getting in the way of their overall performance.

The CEO knew they weren't operating at the right level, but didn't know what needed to be done to get them to do things differently.

In Amy's case, there was so much she didn't know about leading. The group of people who used to be her team were behaving differently once the previous boss left. However, they were also being treated differently, because Amy's style wasn't the same as her boss's.

As a result, she started turning into a control freak – something common in new managers, and very easy not to realise!

This problem emerges due to a lack of trust: in Amy's case, both of herself, as she second-guessed what she should be doing, and of her team.

As time went by, Amy's distrust in the team grew. She had given them space and autonomy to get on with their work without realising that they were used to a more hands-on approach from their previous boss.

So, let's do a quick little check-in.

Ask yourself honestly:
- How are you getting on in your management role?
- Do you find it easier to do everything yourself rather than teaching others what you know?

If, like Amy, you are a perfectionist and a control freak and believe that only you can do the work in the right way, then everything will be harder as you become busier. What's more, you will become more stressed because you are trying to get everything done.

The need to control everything creates even more work.

This is even more problematic if you are managing remote teams and changing working conditions.

In that case, not being able to see your team and what they are doing causes you more stress and anxiety. There is a risk that you will start doing more rather than less because you either don't want to burden your team with more work, or you're not sure they are capable of it.

You will not thrive in this space. In fact, your stress levels can become so high that you're in danger of burning out, jeopardising your career and putting your team at risk.

You will become busier and busier, which has a flow-on impact on your life, your relationships with family and friends, and your health. Your time and energy are always being spent on the small tasks.

---

*This doesn't lift you to the level you
should be operating at in the role.*

LEARNING TO LET GO

I bet when you applied for that promotion you were excited and felt you could do this standing on your head.

And now, here you are doing the role, and you're wondering why it's harder than you expected.

The work you are an expert at is most likely not part of your role now.

A leadership role requires more 'thinking' than the 'doing'-type role you are used to.

When your head is down in the doing, you aren't looking up with a future focus or doing the high-value work appropriate for your new senior level.

What you are being paid to do now is different from what you did in your old role.

That's the thing about leading. The person you were in your old, technical role must morph into another style of person. You need to approach things differently to lead the team well, so that you're all performing at the right level.

This is about letting go of what you used to do.

I'm not saying you must change everything about who you are. Your values, beliefs and core identity will remain unchanged (mostly). It's some of your behaviours, habits and skills that need to level up.

———————————

This leadership role requires new skills, so you must be prepared to become a learner again.

———————————

The skills you developed over time will not necessarily make you successful in this management role.

You have moved on from a role you can do standing on your head, that was easy (in retrospect), and where you probably had some time and flexibility on your hands. Now you are stretched, figuring out what managing others involves, doing your work (and some of your old job), as well as looking after and being responsible for a whole group of people.

You also want to do a great job, which means the 'control freak' part of you may break out and you will start micromanaging your team to ensure the work is done 'right'. Or you will do most of the work yourself, so it will be done the way you like it.

This increases the risk of overwhelm and – at its extreme – burnout.

It's assumed that when people are promoted to management roles, they will 'pick up' how to lead as they go along. However, leading a team requires a whole new set of skills that are difficult to just 'pick up'.

What organisations misunderstand, or neglect, is the need to support managers who are leading from the middle, so they can develop the necessary skills to lead well.

———————————

It's time to change what you are currently doing, step into the learner space to develop some new skills, and evolve your thinking to level up and lead!

———————————

LEVELLING UP

Levelling up means you are focusing on the work appropriate for your pay grade.

Working out what that is can be one of the challenges.

It's about being prepared to:

———————————

*Let go of your perfectionism.
Let go of your need to control everything.
Let go of the need to stay across the smallest details of what your team is doing.*

———————————

Levelling up reduces the risk of feeling overwhelmed and burning out.

Your team wants to be able to learn from you and be inspired to level up as well.

This means moving from being a **Transactional Manager** to a **Transformational Leader**, as shown in *Figure 1.1*.

A TRANSACTIONAL MANAGER	A TRANSFORMATIONAL LEADER
Still doing the tasks from their old role that other people are now employed to do	Understands what they should be doing and what the team should be doing
Thinks there is only one way – their way	Can let go of the technical work and let their team get on with it
Struggles to let go of doing everything	Understands that there are different ways to achieve a result
Disempowers the team	Empowers the team
Doesn't have time to focus on future goals and outcomes	Focuses on meaningful, well-defined goals and outcomes that align with organisational purpose and strategy

Figure 1.1: Transactional versus transformational

If you don't know how to manage and lead a team of people, you are more likely to default to operating as a Transactional Manager and doing the technical tasks from your old role. These feel safer and easier because you're good at them.

But your role now requires high-value thinking, where you focus on future aspirations and goals for the team and how that fits with the organisation's overall strategy and purpose. This is what a Transformational Leader does.

Levelling up means you and your team are heading in the same direction. The team will understand their roles, and you will be able to focus on high-value, future-oriented work.

———————————

You are more strategic and can focus on what you need to do as a team to achieve your outcomes.

———————————

SETTING UP FOR SUCCESS

The benefit of this is that when you step up, you lift your abilities, which will lift your team, and everyone levels up.

You are influencing the direction for the team and can consider what future success looks like.

You understand what your role is and what it isn't. You know that what you used to do, were good at, and liked to do may not be part of your role now.

There is time to develop your team, and to work on other, more important projects appropriate for your role.

Instead of saying, 'I don't have time to train someone,' you understand this is an investment of your time. That investment will pay off for you tenfold.

You know that your team will operate well when you're away.

When you are operating at the right level and doing the work relevant for your pay grade you will still be busy, but not the crazy busy that has had you working twelve-hour days, plus weekends.

Gradually, the time pressures will ease. Work will be more enjoyable. Weekends will become freer and give you a chance to focus on things other than work.

You are starting to create a life by design rather than living a life driven by work.

As you lift, your team will lift. Everyone will start to perform better, be more productive, and focus on what needs to be done.

Your enjoyment and understanding of this role will grow.

You will start to feel that some components of leading are becoming effortless. You are more mindful of your strengths and how you can leverage them to perform in this role even better.

Learning to let go allows you to start to perform your role effectively, tap into your best thinking, and help your team to thrive.

As your team's capability grows, you will have more capacity to focus on the work you should be doing.

You will start to discover that your team is far more capable than you initially thought. They are likely to become more proactive, more collaborative, and more able to take on extra responsibility.

There is no longer a risk of burnout, and you are on your way to brilliance.

———————————

*People management changes from 'fighting fires',
performance-managing, and micromanaging to
encouraging, learning from, and growing with the team.*

———————————

Activity 1.1: The control freak checklist

Tick the boxes that apply to you:
- ❑ You are involved in absolutely everything that your team is working on.
- ❑ You wake up in the middle of the night remembering a specific task that was still outstanding, but you had completely forgotten about.
- ❑ You are going to meetings with stakeholders, and there are several other members of your team also attending.
- ❑ You are writing papers or presentation packs from scratch.
- ❑ You are the liaison point between other areas and your team – for everything.

❏ You are in back-to-back meetings all day with no breaks and no time to do any of the work coming out of those meetings.

❏ You are starting earlier and finishing later to keep on top of things and try to get everything done. You have no time for yourself, let alone your family and friends.

❏ You are not playing to your strengths. You used to love what you did and were very good at doing in your (old) job, but these skills aren't required in this one. You are struggling to understand what you need to do to feel like a success in this role.

❏ You got to where you are now because of your work ethic, yet it seems like this isn't working for you now.

❏ You are a perfectionist, so find it hard to let others take on the work you used to do so well.

❏ At times, you know you are behaving like a control freak and can't let things go. You are afraid that if you don't stay across everything, mistakes will occur.

❏ Your boss has been told by your team that you are micromanaging them. You just want them to do the work right in the first place. Until you know what they are capable of, you must stay across everything they are doing.

❏ You want to be seen as capable in doing this role, so tend to control everything that is going on. Others won't do the work as well as you.

❏ You are so busy reacting to other people and situations that when you get to the end of the day, you find you haven't achieved any of your goals and feel exhausted.

If you have ticked ANY of these boxes, then you are at risk of burnout and overwhelm. And you are demonstrating signs that you are becoming, or have already become, a control freak.

LETTING GO

A case study

Watching MK move from being a control freak to levelling up meant a lot to me. A senior doctor in a major hospital, MK was extraordinarily good at what she did in a very specialised area of health.

Which meant she did everything, even though there was a team in place to do different elements of the work.

MK had become the person managing this disparate and complex team because of her expertise in this field and her drive to move forward.

She had no management skills, and was overwhelmed with the challenges of managing effectively.

MK was not a natural leader. She was very comfortable being a Doer, and would have loved to stay in the space of the technical expert. However, to succeed in what she was trying to achieve, she needed to build a team with the capability to take her initiatives further and to support a larger group of people who needed specialised care.

Her life was out of whack as she spent too much time running the area, organising others, doing rounds, supervising, being the expert, applying for grants, hiring, mediating disputes, dealing with conflict, and so on.

MK's family life was suffering, and her level of exhaustion and frustration was growing.

I felt exhausted just hearing her describe everything she was doing.

It took several months for MK to gradually relinquish control and start tapping into her team's expertise.

This meant she could start to lead more effectively and level up. This began by stepping through a process of:

- Resetting boundaries to move from overwhelm to a level of control,
- Building a safe and connected team by reducing interpersonal frictions, and
- Enhancing communication and relationships to build team connection.

CHAPTER 1 SUMMARY AND ACTIONS

- Being a control freak may make you comfortable in knowing things are being done to your level of detail. But continuing to be one creates overwhelm and exhaustion.
- The thought of learning to let go of perfection may be scary for you, but you can't level up without doing it to some degree.
- Understanding how to level up means you are focusing on the work appropriate for your pay grade.

ACTION

Keep *The control freak checklist* close by and read through it every month or so until you have levelled up and let go of this persona.

It's time to read on and find out how you can create capacity, balance and control in your work. Importantly, this will help you love what you do (again).

CHAPTER 2:

FROM INEFFECTIVE TO TRANSFORMATIONAL LEADER

Samar had moved into a mid-level role in a large organisation. It was an important role in a business area that impacted many other sectors of that organisation. The team was not all in place at the start, and Samar had to hire new members, which took time.

The amount of work was overwhelming as Samar tried to do it all while the team grew. He was across pretty much everything, which made it harder to delegate responsibilities as new team members came on board. Samar's lack of trust in the team, and the fact that he lacked awareness of what they were capable of, meant he held on to everything.

Samar wanted to make sure the work was done 'right'. He also wanted to give the team members time to get up to speed with their respective roles.

This led to things getting dropped, missed, stalled, or forgotten, as Samar was involved in everything but not across everything as thoroughly as he had intended.

The team was struggling as well. They weren't sure what they should be doing, and felt a bit helpless as they watched how busy Samar was.

Samar was frequently stepping into the 'control freak' space, and when he did hand work over to the team he was micromanaging them to do it just as he wanted it done.

Samar was becoming increasingly exhausted, and he couldn't see a way out of this predicament. He was starting work earlier and finishing later, and was playing catch-up on emails on weekends.

It took some time for Samar to learn that he had to start relying on his team more, and that when he handed work over he had to do it in ways that allowed the team to understand what needed to be done.

First, he focused on key areas to learn how to manage the team, and then learnt how to lead them effectively.

'Level up' became Samar's mantra whenever he felt compelled to step in and do something. He started identifying what he was responsible for and what the team was responsible for. He started recognising the difference between transactional work and higher-level work.

Along the way he learnt:
- Just because he *could* do something didn't mean he *should*, and
- His way wasn't the only way to achieve a good result.

———————————

By focusing on learning how to manage and lead, he started tapping into the team's expertise.

———————————

Samar became comfortable letting go of the technical work he was good at and let the team take on more as their capability grew.

By levelling up, Samar is still across everything, but from a higher viewpoint. He knows the team is more than capable, which means they feel more empowered.

He has gone from always feeling overwhelmed by the amount of work to be done, to having the time and mental space to think strategically and focus on meaningful, well-defined goals and outcomes.

Now, instead of feeling overwhelmed, Samar occasionally pauses and thinks, 'What should I be doing right now?' as the transactional work is being managed and done beautifully by his team.

———————————

Your success as a Transformational Leader requires tapping into the often-overlooked brilliance of your team.

———————————

FROM DOING LESS TO BEING MORE

Wrong-level leadership means you are operating at a level (or two) below where you should be. This pushes your team down, so they are operating at a level too low as well. If this phenomenon is widespread across your organisation, then it is not operating as well as it could.

Building awareness of how you operate and what your leadership attributes are will help you work out the skills you need to develop and level up.

When you are operating at the wrong level, your work is controlling you instead of you controlling your work.

Operating at the right level means you become noticed by your boss for all the right reasons. And your boss's boss starts to see how effectively you are managing, and how capable your team is becoming.

Because a rising tide lifts all boats.

As you lift your team will lift, and overall everyone will perform better, be more productive and focus on what needs to be done.

The leaders that make leading look effortless understand their team's capabilities. They know their individual strengths and look at ways to build potential.

You will be giving more autonomy to your team and empowering them to step up and take pride in what they do.

This will enable you to:
- Tap into a greater number of ideas
- Create higher levels of team trust and engagement
- Develop new leaders by allowing team members to take on more responsibility, which prepares them for future leadership roles
- Effectively delegate to your team
- Help build pride and teamwork
- Shift your focus to leading and allow you to spend more time on 'the big picture'
- Capitalise on the unique strengths and abilities of each team member

———————————

You start to move from doing less, to being more.

———————————

As you've seen in Samar's story, failure to step up and lead at the right level creates busyness, overwhelm, and team confusion. Worse yet, if you don't find ways to make space for yourself, let go of your need to do everything, and build team capability, you are at risk of staying an ineffective and Transactional Manager instead of a Transformational Leader, as *Figure 2.1* shows.

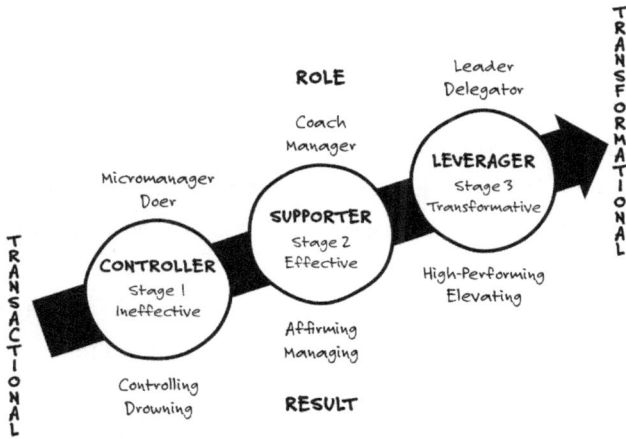

Figure 2.1: The transactional to transformational model

THE THREE STAGES OF LEADERSHIP

Let's look at the three stages to move from being a Transactional Manager who, at the bottom of this model, is operating at a level (or levels) too low. A Transactional Manager is focusing on the detail and the doing, is too involved in the nitty-gritty, and is too controlling of the team.

Moving up this model means becoming a Transformational Leader: someone who leverages the skills of those around them, operates at the level appropriate to their pay grade, and helps their team operate at the right level.

Stage 1
CONTROLLER: Ineffective
This is the stage where managers often find themselves shortly after being promoted into their first management role.

The roles at this stage are **Doer** and **Micromanager**.

As a Doer, you find it hard to let go. You continue to do the tasks you used to do, as it is easier to do them yourself and you believe you do them best. This creates a stressed culture in which the team can't tap into your expertise as you are too busy 'doing'.

The result is that you are drowning at this level. The team is disempowered and unsure of what they should be focusing on.

As a Micromanager, you may genuinely be attempting to hand off work instead of doing it yourself. However, if it's not done as you would do it, you either take it back and do it yourself, or you start hovering over the shoulders of your team members to make sure it is done just as you like it.

You are busy instructing or explaining *how* the work should be done. The result is that you are too controlling.

———————————————

This creates an erratic work culture, as the team isn't quite sure where they stand.

———————————————

One moment they're doing the work, and the next you're telling them it's wrong and how they should do it differently, or you're taking it back and doing it yourself.

If you are still doing your old role (or parts of it) and/or are micromanaging your team to do the work the way *you* would do it, you are currently stuck at the Ineffective Stage of **Controller**.

This means the changes you are making (or not making) won't be pleasant, and your career trajectory will be limited or stalled if you stay here.

Activity 2.1: Controller checklist

Tick 'yes' or 'no' to indicate whether these statements apply to you, to see if you are operating at the Controller level.

STATEMENTS	YES	NO
1. People are constantly interrupting you to ask questions or obtain information.		
2. You have been called, and sometimes call yourself, a control freak.		
3. It takes longer to explain the task than to do it yourself.		
4. You don't trust your team to do the task as well as you would do it.		
5. You often take work back after you have given it to someone because you are frustrated with how long it's taking.		
6. You must redo work that others have already done.		
7. Team members are new, and you want to give them time to come up to speed before you hand any work over.		
8. Mistakes will occur if you don't do it yourself.		
9. There's no one to give this work to.		
10. Even after you hand work over, you stay involved in getting it done.		

If you have ticked the 'yes' box for five or more of these statements, you are likely being a Doer or a Micromanager. You are doing too much and not trusting your team to take on some of your work.

Stage 2
SUPPORTER: Effective

This is the level where I find most managers. At this stage you are working well, your team is taking on more responsibilities, and you have handed over some of your previous work and are feeling more comfortable doing so. You and your team, if rated for end-of-year performance, would be deemed to be doing what is expected. You have achieved a satisfactory outcome.

The roles at this stage are **Manager** and **Coach**.

As a Manager, you are willingly sharing your knowledge and expertise and focusing on developing your team. You are on top of the administrative requirements of managing a team.

As a Coach, you are supporting and affirming. You are curious and want to know what your team thinks about the work they are doing, how they want to do it, and what the outcomes will be. You are coaching individual members of the team to help bring out their best, and supporting them to build their capability.

————————————

You can stay in the Effective Stage and your role will be reasonably secure, but you'll always wonder, 'Is there more?'

————————————

Activity 2.2: Supporter checklist

Tick 'yes' or 'no' to indicate whether these statements apply to you, to see if you are operating at this level.

STATEMENTS	YES	NO
1. You understand the aspirations, knowledge, skills, and abilities of each of your team members.		
2. You are comfortable coaching individual members of your team and drawing out their knowledge and expertise.		
3. You understand the core administrative requirements of managing a team.		
4. You have a good view of what must be done, what can be done later or even cancelled, and who can do what.		
5. Your expertise and tasks from your old role are being distributed throughout the team.		
6. You communicate to create shared understanding in what you are trying to achieve.		
7. You feel comfortable leading the team.		
8. You only occasionally succumb to being a control freak and Micromanager.		
9. You are learning that 'perfectionism' is a state of mind.		
10. You are discovering previously undiscovered gold in what your team can do.		

If you have ticked the 'yes' box for five or more of these statements, you are in pretty good shape. You are getting some time back in your day and starting to trust your team to do a good job.

Stage 3
LEVERAGER: *Transformative*

At this stage you are finding the work is becoming effortless. Don't get me wrong – you will still be busy. But you have that feeling of 'flow'. You and the team are heading in the same direction.

Here, the roles are **Delegator** and **Leader**.

As a Delegator you clearly understand your role, what you should be doing, and what your team should be doing. You are operating at the right level for your seniority.

You know what is required to lift the team, and you continue to build their capability to be able to take on the tasks you are delegating.

The result is: the team is elevated.

As a Leader, you have more time to focus on high-value, future-focused work. You link your strategy to the organisation's overarching strategy.

The result is that the team is high-performing, co-creational and innovative.

Your value to the team and to the organisation increases exponentially.

Even though you are still busy, you have now developed the

core skills to manage your workload and lead your team. When you focus on continuing to refine your skills and the skills of your team, overall performance lifts.

At this level you have more space and time. You have more balance and ease in what you do, and your career opportunities grow.

Activity 2.3: Leverager checklist

Tick 'yes' or 'no' to indicate whether these statements apply to you, to see if you are operating at this level.

STATEMENTS	YES	NO
1.You feel your thinking has lifted and you can see the bigger picture for the team.		
2. You and the team are collaborative and co-creational.		
3. Trust in the team's overall capability is high.		
4. You understand each individual team member's capability and the level of support they require to excel.		
5. You are an effective and Deliberate Delegator.		
6. You are less involved in what the team is doing because they capably do what needs to get done.		
7. Your leadership skills and team achievements are being noticed at senior levels.		

8. You can prioritise and focus on those tasks that have the biggest impact on outcomes and results.		
9. You feel in control and not overwhelmed.		
10. You feel that there are several contenders for promotion in terms of succession planning.		

If you have ticked 'yes' for five or more of these, you are in excellent shape. Your team is engaged and you know that they 'have this'. Everyone is stepping in and doing what they need to do. There is increased productivity, improved motivation, and focus on your team's purpose and outcomes.

Based on this model, where are you at now, and where do you want to be?

SAME, SAME BUT DIFFERENT

When you develop the skills to support your team and tap into what they can bring to their roles, there is an expansion of what you and what your team can do.

The person in that old role has morphed into someone else. A common saying demonstrates this: 'Same, same and a little different.' This means that you are the same person, but with some differences from who you were previously. In this case, those small changes you made have lifted you and your team's abilities.

Your thinking changes as your perception and perspective changes. This happens when you step up and start focusing on managing and leading your team.

You will start to see and hear things differently. Your boss may start to treat you differently. Their expectations of you will change as your experience and skills grow.

———————————

You cannot NOT change. How you do this is up to you.

———————————

Activity 2.4: The 12-months-from-now letter to yourself

I love using the following exercise to identify where you are now, and where you want to end up as a leader.

Creating leadership goals gives you something to aim for. Grab a pen and journal and spend some time identifying what you want to achieve.

Twelve months from now, imagine you are reading this letter.

The letter describes what you want to achieve in terms of becoming a Transformational Leader.

What does it say? What has changed from where you are now? What changes in your leadership style have you implemented?

Use the '5, 4, 3, 2, 1' tool, adapted from Ryder Carroll's book *The Bullet Journal Method.*

The numbers stand for:

- 5 years – tell yourself what you want to achieve in the next 5 years
- 4 quarters – write about what you want to achieve over the next year
- 3 months – what you want to get done in the next quarter
- 2 weeks – what you need to complete in the next 2 weeks
- 1 day – what you must do in the next 24 hours (this is your first step)

Start the letter with:

'Hi there – it's now <date>, 12 months after I started reading *Level Up* by Maree Burgess. These are the aspirations and goals I set for myself then:

5. It is now <date 5 years from now>

I have … or I am …

(What are the goals you want to achieve? What evidence will you have that they are achieved?)

4. It is now <date 4 quarters/12 months from now>

I have … or I am …

and now my leadership skills are …

and my team is …

(What are the goals you want to achieve? What evidence do you have that they are achieved?)

3. It is now <date 3 months from now>
   I have … or I am …
   which means that …
   (What are the goals you want to achieve? What evidence
   do you have that they are achieved?)

2. It is now <date 2 weeks from now>
   I have … or I am …
   which means that …
   (What are the goals you want to achieve? What evidence
   do you have that they are achieved?)

1. It is now <date 1 day from now>
   I have … or I am …
   which is the first step to achieving my other goals.
   (What is that first step? What evidence do you have that
   it is achieved?)

I'm excited to say that I am well on the way to achieving my
5-year goal. I will reset my 12-month goals having met each one.

Signed … <your name>'

As you read through this book, identify the chapters, sections or ideas that will help you achieve what you have written above.

Make a commitment to yourself to start that first step.

Then, identify what the second step is.

Look at number 2 above, your two-week goal. Identify the steps that achieve that and plan it out now.

Look at number 3 above. What do you want to achieve over the next three months? This becomes your 90-day plan. Keep coming back to this letter and update numbers 1, 2, and 3 to maintain momentum.

THE SECRETS OF AN EFFECTIVE LEADER

A case study

From the moment that Sue stepped into a leadership role, her priority was the people.

She has had many people during her career who have helped her to develop her skills. Typically, it was a boss that she worked for who had her back and pushed her along. It has also been people in her team who gave her confidence, and pushed her to do more and do it better.

Having people to support her has been really important to Sue. These individuals include people in her team, the people above her, and her peers who have her back and who have given her support, encouraged her, and helped her build her confidence.

She's done this by focusing on building relationships.

Curiosity, and being prepared to say 'I don't understand', is another key component of Sue's leadership skills.

'There's been plenty of times where I say, "I still don't understand," and I'm comfortable to ask the question ten times to make sure I do,' says Sue. 'I let myself be really vulnerable, and the team values that. I think it's just being real. When you're real, people trust you. If you're putting it on, people can see it a mile off.'

Every time Sue has been promoted, she realises in retrospect that she has changed by default and started thinking differently.

'Taking broader and bigger roles means if you don't change your thinking you'll fail at it. I've done that by pushing myself to take on the challenge. A bigger, broader role feels scary, and sometimes feels too big. Once I've started, I do a lot of asking questions, listening to understand, and respecting different and diverse views.'

Sue has worked with effective teams and transformed them to be high-performing. She has also at times inherited ineffective teams and transformed them to be effective.

I started working with Sue when she stepped into her first leadership role as a mid-level manager. I watched her grow her team and change how *she* operated to be more effective. She levelled up in the role, and I watched the team level up with her.

Sue has recently stepped into a C-suite role reporting to the CEO of a mid-sized organisation, a step she didn't imagine making a few years ago. Her willingness to develop the skills needed at each new level has led to her success. She is the same person I knew years ago – and a little different!

CHAPTER 2 SUMMARY AND ACTIONS

The transactional to transformational model describes the levels at which managers or leaders are operating.

Operating at the ineffective end means you are operating at a level (or two) below where you should be. This pushes your team down, so they are operating at a lower level as well.

Building awareness of how you operate and your leadership attributes will help you work out the skills you need to develop and level up. By doing this, you will lead at the right level and move towards the transformational end of this model.

Learning how to manage and lead means you can start tapping into your team's expertise.

ACTION

- Consider *Figure 2.1: The ineffective to transformational model*. Where are you on this? Are you near the ineffective end or the transformational end? Identify where would you like to be.
- Review the Controller checklist and identify what you need to do to move more of these answers to 'no'. Then review the Supporter and Leveragor checklists

and identify what you need to do to move more of these answers to 'yes'.

- Review the letter to yourself which describes where you want to be in twelve months. Where can you store this so you can find it easily for updates?

It's time to read on and find out how you can level up and lead.

PART TWO

HOW TO LEVEL UP AND LEAD

Now you know where you are in terms of being a Transactional Manager, a Transformational Leader, or somewhere in between.

The next step is to change how you lead and then develop the behavioural skills required to lift both yourself and your team.

Everyone, and I mean everyone, has the potential to level up in some way.

Part Two has three sections: Clear the Decks, Start Your Engines, and Get Underway.

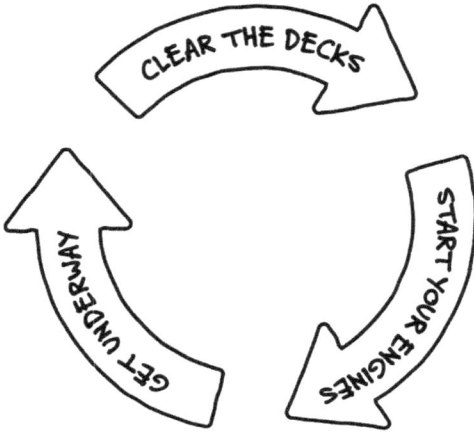

Figure 3.1: Level up and lead

Clear the decks – This is about having an inward focus and working out what is preventing you from leading effectively.

It starts by completing a Task Audit and identifying everything on your mind, putting it down on paper (or a whiteboard), and then putting it in order to start reducing your stress.

Then you will be working on a Mindset Audit, where you will discover more about what makes you tick. The focus here is self-awareness: understanding the leadership attributes required to lead at the right level, and creating confidence to be able to leave things in the team's hands if you're away.

Start your engines – This is about having an outward focus, building your awareness of your team, and learning how to empower them to do more.

Knowing your team is about learning to listen to them, being curious about them, and considering their perspective. Empowering your team is about building their trust, coaching them, and creating stretch opportunities for them.

Get underway – This is about changing how you are communicating.

It starts with identifying if you are a **Doer**, a **Persuader**, a **Supporter** or an **Influencer**.

You will then discover what is required to be a **Deliberate Delegator** and understand the strategies that may trip you up. Most importantly, this section will help you learn how to delegate.

After that, you're ready to learn how to communicate more effectively by following the *8 Ingredients for clear instructions*.

———————————

'A fundamental lesson of leadership is that it's not about you, it's about the people following you. The best leaders focus almost all their energy [on] inspiring and empowering others.'
– Ted De Por, co-founder, Cropsmart

———————————

CHAPTER 3:

CLEAR THE DECKS – INWARD FOCUS

Melinda and I are sitting together for her first coaching session. I had thought about how we would start, and had decided to spend ten minutes or so focusing on what was on her 'to-do' list.

Ninety minutes later I am still filling a very large whiteboard with everything that she was currently doing, had to do, and wanted to do. It became clear that she had too much on her plate. (I bet that sounds familiar!)

Melinda had recently started in a new role, and she was aware of the expectations on her to achieve significant change within her first six months.

She had a lot on her mind, and seeing it all written up on a whiteboard was alarming, yes, but it also highlighted what she needed to prioritise.

Building awareness about what is on your mind is crucial. Dumping everything onto a piece of paper or whiteboard is a way to free up space in your mind.

This is about preparing for action.

It's like sailing. Before setting sail a crew prepares by fastening down or removing all loose objects on the decks in case they get in the way or cause an injury.

Clearing the decks must happen before a leader can step up and lead at the right level and make room for higher-value work.

OPERATING AT THE WRONG LEVEL

Not being aware of everything that's on your mind can be a barrier to taking control of your role. This means you are operating at a level too low and trying to do too much.

This leads to overwhelm, stress and exhaustion. Too much overwhelm creates distress and impacts our health, and it can become a downward spiral as your ability to think clearly diminishes.

Neuroscience research indicates that overwhelm impacts the ability to tap into the part of our brain that allows us to do our best thinking – the pre-frontal cortex. Instead, we can go into survival mode, which means we are relying on the reptilian parts of our brain to protect us.

Melinda demonstrated this when she completed the Control

Freak checklist in the first chapter. She ticked off nearly all of the items.

Being new to her role, Melinda wanted to stay across everything. She was trying to do it all while waiting for her team to come up to speed.

She struggled to identify what she could hand over to the team. She felt that:

- She needed to do everything. This was an important, high-profile, strategic role, and she wanted to succeed in it.
- She was abdicating her responsibility if she gave 'her' work to the team.
- She was letting go of what she should do, and wanted to hold on more tightly to maintain a sense of control.
- She worried others would wonder what she did if she was giving so much to her team.

In her book *Argh! Too Much Information, Not Enough Brain*, Lynne Cazaly describes how repeated, unending overwhelm leads to burnout and health issues. She shares how we need to acknowledge our emotions, manage our workload, and filter the amount of information that threatens to submerge us.

Melinda wasn't at this stage yet, though signs of overwhelm were beginning to emerge.

---

*Right-level leadership is about doing the work
relevant for your pay grade, and your team
doing the work relevant for their pay grade.*

OPERATING AT THE RIGHT LEVEL

You are operating at the right level when:

1. You are aware of what your team is working on, but not down to the tiniest details.
2. You are not doing everything yourself.
3. You are letting go of the work that used to be part of your old role, and focusing on the work required according to your role description.
4. You have reduced the number of meetings you attend, particularly those with representation from your team members.
5. You are reviewing papers or presentation packs for final edits only.
6. Your team is building strong relationships with stakeholders and other areas of your organisation.
7. You may start to find moments in the day when you have nothing to do!

---

*So that's why it's critically important to complete an audit
of everything that's on your mind and your to-do list.*

Reviewing what's on your mind and what's keeping you up at night, like Melinda did, helps with the overwhelm. And you'll have a good idea of what to do now, do later, hand off to someone else, or not do at all.

I used to call the following activity 'defragging your brain'. 'Defrag' is an old computer term used back in the day that refers to cleaning up computers to create space. Not many people know this term any more. These days, I have a 'Clean My Mac' app that cleans up system junk, empties the trash, and optimises speed on my MacBook, so maybe I should call this a 'Clean My Brain' app!

But instead, I'm calling the activity a Task Audit.

AUDIT YOUR TASKS

As a leader, you are probably wearing too many hats and trying to do too much. If you're new to this role, you may still be focusing on work from your old role, either because you love the work or you don't yet have anyone else to take it on.

It's not sustainable to keep doing everything. You must learn to do things differently.

That starts with taking inventory and making a list of all the things that you feel you need to do, so that you can really focus on what is filling your calendar, cluttering your day, and filling your mind.

A Task Audit is a key step to clearing the decks.

This means downloading everything that is in your mind that you are doing, thinking about doing, need to do, or want to do.

You are not indispensable, although you may be in the short term, and that puts your team and organisation at risk.

A lot of people (and their bosses) have an unrealistic belief about how much they are expected to do.

After completing a Task Audit, you must consider each item. Which of these:

- Do you need to keep because only you have the required expertise to do this work?
  Note: Anything you are keeping must have a high value and a future focus.
- Can you delegate either to people in your team, other areas within the organisation, or even to external contractors? As you think about each task or project on the list, ask yourself: *'Who could do this task if not me?'*
- Can be planned and diarised for a future date?
- Do you typically get caught out with at the last moment and need to respond to?
- Can you plan for rather than getting caught out each time. Be proactive rather than reactive.
- Can you delete from the list because it doesn't need to be done at all?

- Do you struggle with because they do not play to your strengths?

It's time to start clearing the decks and handing over work. See *Activity 3.1.*

---

*You're on your way to freedom from
never having to do this again.*

Activity 3.1: Task Audit template

Make a list of all the tasks you are currently doing that are part of your role, and those that aren't.

These tasks include everything that is filling your calendar, sitting at the back of your mind, cluttering your life, and making you procrastinate.

Include the repetitive things you do on a daily, weekly and monthly basis. Imagine if you weren't around to complete this work: you might be on holidays, away for a family emergency, attending a child's school camp, on unexpected health leave, and so on.

Some examples of repetitive tasks might include:
- Routine meetings
- Email responses/management

- Bookkeeping
- Social media creation/management
- Generating reports
- Marketing projects
- Accounting
- Preparing presentations/board papers
- Travel and itineraries

In the table below, tick the column that identifies if the task will be kept or not. What can be delegated? Is it something you typically react to, when planning may be required instead?

Start by picking one task you have identified to delegate. Who in your team is the best person to give some of this work to?

Pick another task and identify who could do it, and so on.

If a task adds no value, cross it off the list, or outsource it to another area or another organisation.

TASKS	KEEP	DELEGATE	PLAN

Now that you've completed a Task Audit, everything that was in your head is written down in front of you. You have a good idea of what you need to do, and a more realistic sense of how much you were expecting yourself to do.

No wonder you felt exhausted and tired! Just looking at that list would be overwhelming.

Remember:

———————————

Just because you CAN do something doesn't mean you SHOULD.

———————————

Louise learnt this, and it changed how she operated.

When we met, Louise was struggling with her workload after being promoted.

We had dived into her Task Audit and discovered there was a big chunk of work she was doing that wasn't part of her new, senior role.

It was a component of her previous role that she loved, and wasn't willing to hand over. This particular task was something Louise was very good at, and no one else knew how to do it.

After some convincing, she identified two people in the team to train in this aspect of her work, and agreed to let it go.

Delegation can be extremely challenging when we must let go of work we love to do. We may feel like we are losing part of our identity.

A key aspect of stepping into more senior roles is the willingness to change and grow.

Once Louise moved the work on, she could focus on the strategic and high-value work she had been promoted to do.

Stay accountable

A key thing to remember is that even though you may be assigning a task, a project, or an ongoing operational piece to someone else, you must remain accountable for that work (unless it shouldn't have been on your list in the first place).

One of two things can happen when you delegate:

1. Being accountable for someone else's work creates anxiety and impatience for both parties. Some of your 'control freak' habits may emerge to ensure that this work is done as you would do it. This means the person you have assigned to do the work may feel undue pressure to do it as you expect.
2. It can provide an opportunity to work together, transform ideas, and co-create new ones. You are comfortable that the person doing this work has it well in hand. You've provided clear instructions, and you have both checked for shared understanding of what is expected. This opens opportunities for new ideas and new ways of doing things to emerge. There may be pressure, but it is a good pressure to get the best results.

This second possibility enables you to level up, delegate, and create accountability by lifting team capability. Staying aware of this will make you more sensitive to what your team is experiencing and allow you to support them to do their best.

It isn't possible to lead a team of any size and do all the work yourself. If you do, you and the team will start to implode, and will ultimately fail.

Being able to let go of 'your' way of doing something and allow your team to come up with *their* way is essential.

———————————

This means staying open to what you may perceive as imperfection.

———————————

AUDIT YOUR MIND

Next, it's time to complete a Mindset Audit, which is about understanding what makes *you* tick.

It involves:

1. Being aware of yourself. Why you do some things and not others; why you resist change in some areas and not others; what beliefs you hold, and which of those are limiting you in some way; what values drive you and how they align with the values of your organisation.

2. Understanding leadership attributes. These attributes are required by leaders who focus on high-value, future-focused work. This is where leaders are leading at the right level and helping their team level up.

3. Creating capacity to take time off (seriously!). This is about understanding what is required to take leave and know that your area will operate efficiently while you are away.

Let's look at each in detail now.

1. Being aware of yourself

When I look at successful leaders, time and again I find that it's their awareness of themselves that has given them the edge. Self-awareness is about having a strong sense of who you are; you understand and can predict your emotional reactions to situations.

You are putting your attention inward, focusing on what makes you tick.

The more you know about yourself, the more you are able to start becoming the type of leader you strive to be.

This includes knowing the limiting beliefs or fears you hold.

The list of limiting beliefs and fears below are examples that I come across time after time that can prevent the leaders I work with from clearing the decks.

Activity 3.2: Limiting beliefs checklist

Tick those beliefs that apply to you:

- ❑ Every team member is busy, and you don't want to burden them more.
- ❑ New team members need to come up to speed before you can hand them work.
- ❑ You don't trust your team to do the work like you do.
- ❑ It takes longer to explain how to do something than it does to do it yourself.
- ❑ If a task is menial, you can't pass it on.
- ❑ If you pass work on, you'll become obsolete.
- ❑ You like to be the only one who knows how to do something.
- ❑ You are more important when you hold specific knowledge.
- ❑ If the team is better at something than you, it will make you look bad.
- ❑ You don't know how to be strategic, so best to keep busy doing other things.
- ❑ The team believes you are passing on your grunt work.
- ❑ Mistakes occur when you don't do certain work yourself.
- ❑ It's quicker to do it yourself.
- ❑ It's easier to do it yourself.
- ❑ You don't know what to hand over.

What other beliefs have you thought of?

- ❑ _____

☐ _____
☐ _____

Beliefs affect your behaviour, but once they are identified and dealt with they start to lose their power over you. Sometimes evidence that we can do something is all that is needed. Just try doing it. Once proven wrong, the belief will change instantly and lose its influence over you.

Pausing and thinking about what you are resisting helps you to understand more about what makes you who you are.

Limiting beliefs can prevent you from changing or trying something new. They are usually outside of your conscious awareness, meaning you don't even know that they exist.

These beliefs are often based on assumptions that are not true or not tested enough. For instance, a belief that 'you can't delegate' may start as an assumption that becomes true. Perhaps you tried to delegate something unsuccessfully in the past, so best not to delegate anything else.

Limiting beliefs can change.

By identifying and understanding your beliefs, which are at the core of who you are, you can use them or change them to guide your decisions and behaviour.

The more understanding and control you have over your beliefs, the more choice you create for yourself.

Imagine if your goal is to reduce overwhelm. Questions to help identify and change limiting beliefs that may contribute to this include:

- What is preventing you from achieving your goal?
- What are the beliefs you hold that support this?
- Where do you think these beliefs stem from? (Think about major events in your life and what beliefs may have taken root because of them.)
- Consider one of these limiting beliefs. What would you need to do to remove or diminish this limiting belief and create a more empowering one?
- What are some empowering beliefs that will help you reach this goal? Empowering beliefs help you make changes and reach decisions confidently.

Understanding what makes you tick helps you understand what makes other people tick. We all have our own distinct model of the world. The differences between how I see the world and how you see the world can often create misunderstanding. The more understanding you have about this, the more opportunity you have to reduce misunderstanding.

Self-awareness is a lifelong pursuit.

There are many ways to expand your self-awareness and there are various tools you can use, some of which I have listed below. Search online to find out more information about these. You will find free surveys for some of them.

- **MBTI** (Myers-Briggs Type Indicator). Developed by Katharine Briggs and Isabel Briggs Myers early in the 20th century, this highly regarded tool identifies our preferences in how we experience the world. Personality-type information enhances your understanding of yourself, your motivations, your natural strengths, and your potential areas for growth. MBTI introduces you to key areas of strength, communication preferences, relationship preferences, leadership styles, behaviour patterns, and even career choices. Many organisations use MBTI to help teams understand how they work (or don't work) together.

- **People Styles**. Developed by Robert Bolton and Dorothy Grover Bolton, this is also a simple yet powerful tool to identify differences between people. It is based on the notion that all people exhibit one of several different behavioural 'styles'. These differences can often be a major source of friction. It describes how and why we relate more effectively with some people than others. Understanding what people style you are and the people styles of those you work with will help you manage and enhance relationships.

- **VIA (Values in Action) Survey of Character Strengths**. Developed by Christopher Peterson and Martin Seligman in the early 2000s, this is a free self-assessment that provides information to help you understand your best qualities. Seligman and Peterson found that people have more potential for growth when they invest energy in developing their strengths instead of only correcting their weaknesses. Discovering your strengths means you can use them to face life's challenges, work towards goals, and feel more fulfilled both personally and professionally.

- **Clifton Strengths Assessment**. Developed by Don Clifton after his return from World War II, this tool is founded on the question: 'What would happen if we studied what was right with people versus what's wrong with people?' This assessment focuses on helping people maximise their potential to understand not only who they are, but who they can become. It helps you discover your natural talents and what you do best.

Another easy (and free!) way to know your strengths is to simply ask people what they think your strengths are. Also think about your accomplishments, moments of pride and great performances.

_____

When you know your strengths you're more likely to infuse your work with meaning and passion, and to have more impact.

_____

What do you value?

Your values are the things you believe are important in the way you live and work.

They (should) determine your priorities, and deep down they're probably the measures you use to tell if your life is turning out the way you want it to.

When the things you do and the way you behave match your values, life is usually good. You're satisfied and content. But when the things you do don't align with your personal values, that's when life feels difficult and even wrong.

If you are not aware of your values, you tend to be blind to what's going on both within you and around you. You may be more likely to misinterpret others, react unconsciously rather than consciously, and send the wrong messages. This inevitably leads to less desirable outcomes, which undermines your confidence.

'It's not hard to make decisions when
you know what your values are.'
– Roy Disney

Values are a set of standards that determine attitudes, choices and actions. They are like a compass that guides your life, often functioning at an unconscious level, but guiding you nonetheless.

Values are principles or qualities that you consider important, such as honesty, education or hard work.

They reflect who you are, not what you would like to be.

When you live by your values, life is fulfilling and feels in flow.

When you don't honour your values, you can feel anxious. For example, if you value integrity and you are asked to cover up for a colleague at work, this will cause stress. You may not consciously be aware that it goes against one of your values, but you will sense the discomfort.

Workplaces are becoming more collaborative, and people are increasingly looking for jobs in organisations whose values and culture align with their own. By the same token, the most effective organisations attract people who already share their key values.

It is worth the effort to identify your values. Use the exercise below to start this process.

Activity 3.3: Identifying your values

When what you do and the way you behave match your values, life and work are usually good. When these don't align, you may feel unhappy and not know why.

The following questions help to clarify your values:
- What must you have in your life to feel fulfilled?
- What are the values you absolutely must honour or a part of you dies?
- What values do you see in your own life?
- What values do you tend to sell out on first?
- Where do your values show up?
- Which values are sometimes neglected?
- What are your wants versus your needs?
- When do you automatically say yes or no?

- Where do you limit yourself?
- If you didn't limit yourself, what might you do? (What value would that uphold?)
- Where are you too comfortable?
- What are you willing to risk?
- What will free you up?

This values exercise is a useful way to discover the relative importance of each of your values.

1. Using the questions above, start by asking: 'What is important in my life?' For example, these may be things like honesty, being calm, risk-taking, achievement, equality, and so on. Then continue to explore this by asking: 'What else is important in my life?' Keep identifying what you value until you have up to twenty values listed.

2. Now, start narrowing down your list and circle the top eight values that are essential to satisfy you in your work and life.

When narrowing down your values, ask yourself the following questions:
- Does this define me?
- Is this who I am at my best?
- Is this a filter that I use to make hard decisions?

3. You might find that you can chunk words together or clarify meaning for yourself, as some values may be similar.

4. Rank your eight important values by asking: 'Is one more

important than two?', 'Is one more important than three?' and so on. Put a mark against the value that is most important.

5. Write out the top values and define what they mean to you.

To help you with this, think about your key life decisions. It could be when you changed jobs, moved to a new house, started or left a relationship, and so on.

In reflecting on these key moments, consider which values were being either honoured (or not) at that point.

Consider the values that fuelled the decision-making.

You may be surprised when you compare your values this way. Values you may have thought were very important might be further down your hierarchy than you first realised.

6. Looking at your final list, would you be comfortable and proud to tell your values to people you respect and admire?

Do these values represent things you would support, even if your choice isn't popular and puts you in the minority? Are you proud of your top two values?

7. The final step is to identify the behaviours that bring these values to life. How do you need to behave to know that you are living these values?

2. Leadership attributes

Leaders who want to lead at the right level and focus on high-value work with a future focus must have certain leadership attributes.

If you haven't been given any leadership development, then you will fall back on old habits of interacting with others using attributes you have learnt from previous bosses.

If these are effective, then you're off to a good start. If, however, they aren't working for you or your team, then you need to do things differently.

———————————

High-value, future-focused thinking is about being able to step up, take a broader view, and move into the future from the present.

———————————

What makes sense today may mean something else when you consider it from the viewpoint of tomorrow or six months from now.

Ronald Heifetz and Marty Linsky developed the metaphor 'balcony and dance floor' in their book *The Practice of Adaptive Leadership*.

Imagine you are dancing on the dance floor. You are focused on how you're moving, the music that is playing, and the movement of the people around you.

The music finishes and you go upstairs, onto the balcony. Now you can observe everything from a different perspective. You can see the pattern of the dancers down on the floor. You may notice there is a bar downstairs that you didn't notice when you were down there before. You can't see these things when you are on the dance floor.

As a leader, your ability to move from the dance floor to the balcony and back again continuously helps to build your awareness of where your attention is and where it should be for best results.

You may need to be on the dance floor with your team, getting involved in what is going on. And then you may need to step up onto the balcony for that bigger viewpoint.

This is about maintaining perspective during the busyness of doing. Getting off the dance floor and going to the balcony allows you to step back and consider the bigger picture.

Succumbing to busyness and staying stuck on the dance floor does not allow you to gain the perspective and insight required that time on the balcony will bring.

———————————

You need to find time to move away from the action.

———————————

This leads to becoming more behaviourally adaptable and able to readily adjust as situations change.

Start to identify what it would take for you to become the type of leader you aspire to be.

Activity 3.4: Are you leading at the right level?

The following questions and statements will give you an idea of whether you are operating at the right level, or if you are spending too much time on the dance floor.

Tick 'yes' or 'no' as they apply.

QUESTIONS	YES	NO
1. Are people constantly interrupting you to ask questions or obtain information?		
2. Do you spend too much time on the details rather than on strategic planning and staff development?		
3. Do you find it hard to limit the number of projects you are involved in?		
4. Do you find it difficult to say 'no', and are you often doing work for others that they should be doing themselves?		
5. Do you become involved in projects after you have delegated them to someone else?		

If you have answered 'yes' more often, then you may need to consider if you are sabotaging your efforts to lead at the right level.

Now consider these statements, and again tick 'yes' or 'no' as they apply.

STATEMENTS	YES	NO
1. You feel your thinking has lifted and you can see the bigger picture and future impacts for your team.		
2. You regularly review project goals and schedules for you and your team and assess if you need to be involved.		
3. You know how to take a step back to see the bigger picture. For example, you are aware of what is happening across your team and the impact that has on future results.		
4. You trust that the team's overall capability has increased. You are aware of where and how the most successful connections are happening.		
5. You understand what the team needs from you that they're unable to see and ask for.		
6. You regularly bring people from the team up onto the balcony with you by helping them understand the rationale behind their work, reviewing project goals, and being transparent about the organisation's goals.		

More 'yes' answers than 'no' answers mean you are more likely to move readily between the dance floor and the balcony and spend time leading at the right level.

3. Taking time off

Up to now, as a control freak, you are unlikely to take much time off. There is too much to do and only you know how to do it.

Once you build on your self-awareness and dispel some limiting beliefs, you can take time off and know that your team will operate well when you're away.

You don't need to take your phone and laptop with you. It's okay to be unreachable. Really!

You have left the place in good hands. Your team and boss are comfortable that you are away, and you know the area will continue to operate as well as if you were present.

Getting to this level is comforting. Imagine if you had to take an unexpected week off from work. You would know that things will continue to progress. When you do return from planned or unexpected leave, there is hardly any stuff that requires your immediate attention and action.

Conversely, if you haven't taken the time to do this, you may struggle to take time off and may face unexpected consequences when you return, as happened with one of my clients.

Jill returned from leave to discover that the individuals in her team had multiple disagreements. This meant her boss had to keep stepping in to intervene, and several projects hadn't progressed because they were waiting on her input.

Up to then, she had been the buffer between team members when they misbehaved or disagreed with each other.

This team was operating as a group of individuals without regard for each other or what was best for the team. They were only interested in getting the best outcomes for themselves. This became even more evident when Jill was on leave.

When this behaviour was pointed out to her, she started to identify the work she should be doing and what her team should be doing, and redistributing her workload accordingly.

As a team, they identified development areas and worked at building more trust, engagement and collaboration with each other.

Knowing your work will progress and your team will operate well while you're away will signify how far you have come. Awareness and development of your leadership potential and the potential of your team will extend your presence and lift your team to new levels.

Activity 3.5: Efficiency when you are away

Use this checklist to set yourself and your team up for success while you're away.

QUESTIONS	YES	NO
1. Have you completed a Task Audit for what needs to keep going while you're away?		
2. Have you identified who will be acting in your role (second in charge)? Name: _____ Have you briefed them about expectations, authority and tasks?		
3. Have you provided an update to your boss about what will be happening in your absence and who is responsible?		

4. Have you communicated to your team about what is happening during your absence? Do they know the key people to contact if there is an emergency?		
5. What meetings have you booked that are happening in your absence? Will these need to go ahead? Do you need to cancel or delegate? If delegating to someone, does that person have the required information to chair the meeting and progress the agenda?		
6. Write down the meetings you are expected to attend. Do you need a representative to attend? Name: _____ Have you let the organisers know that you are a) not attending, and b) sending a delegate? Have you briefed the delegate with the necessary information to act in your place, and given them the necessary authority to make decisions?		
7. Have you identified all the deliverables due while you are away? If so, who is responsible for them? Name: _____		
8. Have you set up an email out-of-office message telling people who to contact in your absence?		
9. Is there anything else you need to consider in preparation? _____ _____		

LOOKING TO THE FUTURE

A case study

To wrap up this chapter, let's go back to our story of Melinda.

I recently caught up with her in one of our regular meetings. She still had the same huge whiteboard in her office. It was neatly filled with lists of work to be done.

When Melinda saw me looking at it, she said, 'Remember our first session where we filled this with the amount of work I was trying to do, and how overwhelmed I felt? Now this is everything my team is working on, which I'm staying across at a high level.'

'My day-to-day is so different now,' she continued. 'In fact, there are times during the day when I look around and have nothing to do! My team has developed in many areas and truly stepped up to take on more and more responsibility.'

'I now have time to focus on building the external relationships that are critical to my role.'

That's exactly what will happen to you too.

Don't become a leader who is doing work below their pay grade.

Delegate down so you can step up.

CHAPTER 3 SUMMARY AND ACTIONS

Stepping into the Transformational Leader space requires you to clear the decks. This means building your awareness.

1. Being aware of yourself
Why you do some things and not others; why you resist change in some areas and not others; what beliefs you hold, and which of those are limiting you in some way. What values drive you and how they align with the values of your organisation.

2. Understanding leadership attributes
Certain attributes are required by leaders who want to be transformative and concentrate on high-value, future-focused work. These leaders are leading at the right level and helping their team level up.

3. Being able to take time off
This is about understanding what is required to take leave and know that your area will operate efficiently while you are away.

ACTION

- Use *Activity 3.1: Task Audit template* to 'defrag' your mind and start to reduce the overwhelm you are experiencing.

- Complete *Activity 3.2: Limiting beliefs checklist* to identify what is preventing you from reducing the overwhelm.
- Expand your self-awareness: use the tools mentioned in this chapter or ask the people around you what they see as your strengths and best traits of leadership.
- Use *Activity 3.3: Identify your values* to see how your key values play out in your role.
- Leadership attributes – consider where you spend your time. Are you most often on the dance floor and busy in the doing? Or are you on the balcony overseeing what is going on? Use Activity 3.4: Are you leading at the right level?
- When you take time off, are you able to leave your phone and computer at the office? Use *Activity 3.5: Efficiency when you are away* to check that you have everything in place to do so.

It's time to read on and find out how you can start your engines.

CHAPTER 4:

START YOUR ENGINES – OUTWARD FOCUS

I worked with Alice when she first became a manager. She had a team of four, half of whom were contractors. We were growing rapidly, and within six months the team numbered forty people.

With our rapid growth, the recruitment process – which included getting job descriptions written, approved, and advertised, and then interviewing applicants – took time. And it all pretty much fell to Alice.

When she wasn't busy with recruiting, Alice was running from meeting to meeting. When she did have time to work at her desk, there was always a queue of people waiting to ask her questions as they worked to find their feet in their new roles.

Alice would stop what she was doing, ask what they needed, listen to them, and then give them the answer. Which was great, except that every time she was interrupted, she had to take time to refocus on what she had been working on. Then, before she knew it, she would be running to the next meeting.

Her desk was a mess, work was slow or didn't progress while people waited for the chance to ask her what to do next, and she wasn't focusing on what she needed to complete.

She was getting further behind and struggling to stay on top of all the people-management requirements and step up into her new responsibilities.

I started to challenge Alice about how she was responding to the queue of people at her desk. I suggested she stop just giving them answers and become curious about what solution they had thought of first.

This was a struggle, as Alice was the subject-matter expert and had the answers. In fact, in her old role, she was *expected* to have the answers. At first, she couldn't understand how doing this would be useful, as it was much faster to just give the answer.

The team was the engine, but that engine had stalled and was not going very well. Team members couldn't excel while they were waiting for Alice to answer their questions. Starting the engines meant tapping into the team's potential.

As she started asking more questions and becoming genuinely curious about what the other person thought, it became a little easier. Often, the questions alone were enough to set the direction for that person. If not, Alice would follow up and challenge them to consider other ideas or think about the problem from a different perspective.

Over time, the queue of people asking questions at Alice's desk reduced.

I knew she was onto a winner when I saw the person who was most often at her desk asking questions start to make their way over, pause, shake their head, and then turn around and go back to their own desk.

By empowering the team, Alice was tapping into their skills and knowledge and getting more done.

_____

Helping your team to work out answers for themselves is exactly what happens when you learn to ask them questions instead of giving them the answers they are seeking.

_____

Getting to really know your team

In this example, Alice was starting to coach her team to think for themselves and discovering more about them in the process. She was starting to understand more about their strengths and capabilities, and encouraging them to step up and take on more responsibility.

As she started to understand what the team could do, Alice could let go of her need to control everything, which meant she could focus on more high-level work relevant to her role.

If you have been promoted from within your team, you may not know what each member of the team is capable of.

If it is a transactional rather than a high-performing team, each team member will have little awareness of what everyone else is doing or what their peers' skills are. The team is a group of individuals operating mostly independently.

———————————

There is little cohesion, collaboration or co-creation.

———————————

The team is functioning, but it is not thriving.

When you work with someone for some time, or hire someone new, there is a boundary around them called a 'job description'. You start to identify them by their role and overlook the vast potential they have, which they don't often get a chance to show.

You know each other by your job description – what you do day-to-day. You don't always know what else your team members are capable of.

In my experience, there are vast amounts of untapped potential in organisations.

You may not think to ask what else your team members can do, or what else they have done.

One of my clients told me that she almost missed a huge career opportunity because of this. She happened to discover that her organisation was about to hire an expert to meet a particular need.

She had the exact skills and experience they needed, and told her CEO that she could do this, as it was something she had done in an old role with a different organisation. This led to a significant promotion for her.

As the new leader of a team, you have an opportunity to tap into this hidden potential.

This is where you should get curious. What are your team members' strengths and capabilities? What expertise do they have that you may not be aware of? What have they done in the past that would be useful in this team?

When you know more about your team members' capabilities, you can empower them to do more.

Empowering leads to engagement

The more you know about each of your team members, the more you can work out the best tasks to give them.

Like Alice above, empowering others starts with coaching: asking them questions, listening to them, and being curious about their responses.

As you do this, engagement increases, there is more collaboration between team members, and the level of trust within your team grows.

When you completed your Task Audit in the previous chapter, you may have discovered key pieces of work that required dedicated time or a particular skill set.

As you discover more about your team, you find out who can be, and wants to be, challenged by doing different work. If they are looking to develop a specific capability that this work will help with, then give it to them. Help them build the capability. I like to call this 'stretching' them – but in a good way.

Stretch assignments are pieces of work that broaden someone's perspectives and skills, and may be separate from their normal role.

Building your awareness of your team members, their skills, and what they are capable of, and then stretching them to develop new skills means you can start to create space for yourself and get some time back.

As the capability of the team grows you can focus on other work, commit to working more reasonable hours, and stop trying to do everything yourself.

Your curiosity, interest in, and awareness of others builds trust with them. It allows conversations to flow to all sorts of areas and new thinking to emerge. This leads to a team that is more capable and can get more done.

Working in an environment like this is enjoyable. Everyone's work begins to feel more rewarding.

————————————

As you become more effective at doing this, achievements for the team will start to multiply.

————————————

Putting your attention and focus outward on the team helps you to build more understanding of their capabilities and how you can empower them to step up into their roles even more.

This next section describes the two key ways in which you can do this.

1. Know your team
- Listen
- Be curious and ask questions
- Thrive on uncertainty
- Consider their perspective

2. Empower your team
- Build trust
- Coach them
- Provide stretch opportunities

KNOW YOUR TEAM

How much do you know about each of your team members? Asking yourself this question doesn't mean you have to know everything about them and their personal lives.

It does mean understanding things like their career aspirations, what roles they've had in the past, achievements that they are proud of, and so on.

————————————

Building your awareness of your team is something you can become better at because it's a learnable skill.

————————————

Activity 4.1: Know your team checklist

The following checklist helps identify how well you know your team and ways to discover more about them.

These questions can also be used in one-on-one conversations with your team members.

- For this individual, what are their key strengths and capabilities?

  These may be things that you have observed or ones they have identified.

  Some examples: being assertive, running a meeting, being analytical, making complex ideas easy to understand, preparing presentations, building relationships with stakeholders, using advanced Excel spreadsheeting.

- What are their career aspirations?

  Do you know what they want to do in their next role or later in their career?

START YOUR ENGINES – OUTWARD FOCUS 93

- What is their hidden (untapped) potential? What can you uncover that neither you nor they may be aware of?
- How do they like to operate?
  For example, do they need lots of time to prepare and focus on a task? Are they someone who loves detail, or are they a big-picture thinker? Do they like working with people, or do they prefer to work alone? Do they prefer to operate autonomously, or do they need lots of guidance?
- When do they feel appreciated at work?
  In their book *The 5 Languages of Appreciation in the Workplace: Empowering Organizations by Encouraging People*, Gary Chapman and Paul White identify five ways that people feel appreciated or valued in the workplace:

Being told they are doing a good job (words of affirmation); having things done for them (acts of service), being given gifts as a thank-you (gifts of appreciation); having one-on-one time to learn as much as they can (quality time); and being tapped on the shoulder (physical touch).

Listen

In his book *Deep Listening*, Oscar Trimboli says that awareness is all about how we listen to others: listening for both what's being said, and what's not being said.

Done well, listening is a full-body experience:

- Listening with your ears and hearing what others are saying.
- Listening with your eyes and seeing people's body language and facial expressions.

- Listening with your body and feeling sensations based on what you are hearing.

This awareness opens your radar and allows you to gather more data.

Most often, we listen to judge or reject. Or, we are listening for the pause, so we can jump in and say what we need to say. Stephen R. Covey, in *The 7 Habits of Highly Effective People*, says to 'seek first to understand … then to be understood.' This is listening with empathy.

I use an activity in workshops where I ask people to pair up and share a story about a moment in their life that means something to them.

Afterwards, each partner is asked to identify the underlying point of the other's story and determine what they are passionate about.

I share a story about the time I had to care for my sons' bearded dragon lizards while the boys were away camping over Easter.

Now, I hate handling lizards or anything scaly, but felt that I could manage this.

Except that on the day they left, one lizard's leg was badly bitten by a larger lizard, and required veterinary attention. This meant driving for over an hour to a lizard specialist and then applying antibiotics every four hours for over a week, which required me to hold the lizard in one hand while trying to stick a syringe in its mouth. The good news is that the lizard (and its leg) survived.

When I tell this story in my workshop and ask the participants what I am passionate about, they usually correctly identify that I am passionate about my children and will do pretty much anything for them, including holding a cold, scaly reptile multiple times a day.

Listening deeply allows us to tap into more than just the words the other person is saying.

When was the last time you listened to someone to really understand what they were saying – not to judge, or confirm what you were already thinking, or reject what they were saying, but really *listened* to their words, watched their body language, and developed an awareness of them?

———————————

Listening deeply builds our understanding of others.

———————————

Activity 4.2: Listening

Before speaking or responding in a one-on-one with a team member, take a breath, pause, and ask yourself:
- 'Have I heard the other person?'
- 'Do I understand what they are saying?'
- 'Is what I'm about to say worth it?'
- 'Will what I say empower them, or diminish them?'

- 'Am I waiting for them to pause so I can jump in to tell them what I need to tell them?'
- 'Am I leading them to the response I want, or am I open to hearing their ideas?'

You will discover that most of the time, while your comments will probably be right, they may not be worth saying.

Stay in the listening space.

This will empower your team and reduce your need to add value. It lets them take ownership of their work and build commitment for decisions.

'They [some leaders] can talk brilliantly, with a great breadth of knowledge, but they're not very good at asking questions. So, while they know a lot at a high level, they don't know what's going on way down in the system. Sometimes they are afraid of asking questions, but what they don't realize is that the dumbest questions can be very powerful. They can unlock a conversation.'
– Michael J. Marquardt, Leading with Questions

Be curious and ask questions

Develop the art of asking powerful, compelling, sometimes even provocative questions. Questions are invitations into the world of curiosity, and can lead to deep understanding.

This includes questioning what's 'normal', and those people who say, 'This is how we've always done it,' or 'We've tried this before and it didn't work.' Great questions to challenge statements such as these include:

- Why can't we change how it's done?
- What if our assumptions were not true?
- What if the opposite were true?
- What other alternatives would work?
- How might we do it differently?

Consider whether you are asking because you already know the answer, or because you are curious about what the other person's answer could be.

Thrive on uncertainty

While uncertainty can make you feel uncomfortable, sitting in that feeling until it starts to ease can lead to lasting positive experiences.

———————————————

Build a sense of curiosity – ask, don't tell.

———————————————

Be open to sharing what you are thinking so that people start to understand why you have so many questions.

When you ask a good question, you give the other person an opportunity to search through their experiences and find answers they may not have known they had. Answers aren't found in familiar territory. If they were, you'd already have found them.

Questions expand the person's model of the world. Even if they answer 'I don't know,' they had to examine their experiences to respond that way.

—————————————

When you are asking questions from a state of curiosity, it creates a genuine impression in the other person that you want to know more about something.

—————————————

Curiosity is a state of active interest. It's about being open to uncertainty or unfamiliar experiences. It helps you raise awareness of both yourself and others by allowing you to form more satisfying relationships as you demonstrate openness and ingenuity.

When you are curious about others, you will naturally ask more questions because you want to learn more about them.

Your powers of observation expand when you are curious, and you see things differently.

Studies have shown that high levels of curiosity are connected to greater analytic ability, problem-solving, and overall intelligence.

So, focusing on strengthening your curiosity makes you smarter!

Being curious allows you and others to discover new things or new ways of doing something. In contrast, being certain means that you feel you are right, which doesn't allow opportunities for you or your team to explore different ideas.

As Albert Einstein once said:

_____

*'Most teachers waste their time by asking questions which
are intended to discover what a pupil does not know,
whereas the true art of questioning has for its purpose to
discover what the pupil knows or is capable of knowing.'*

_____

Asking questions is about stepping into wonder. Wondering allows you to explore other people's thinking, and is a key ingredient for building trust.

You want to be curious, discover what others are thinking, and expand both your understanding of the world and theirs.

_____

*Practice and develop the art of asking powerful,
compelling, and sometimes provocative questions.*

_____

Consider their perspective

They say you can't really understand another person's experience until you've walked a mile in their shoes – or, in other words, imagined the world from their perspective.

This is where you (metaphorically) step into the other person's shoes and understand the perspective of:

- Who they are,
- What they are interested in,

- What they are capable of,
- Their strengths,
- Their career aspirations, and
- Their potential.

The Perceptual Positions technique helps you do this by building awareness from three points of view.

Viewpoint One: You look at the world through your own eyes, hear with your own ears, and feel, taste and smell using your own senses. Your own point of view, beliefs and assumptions influence your perspective.

Viewpoint Two: You imagine being in the other person's shoes, experiencing what they may be feeling and seeing. Matching their breathing pattern, posture and voice helps you to imagine their point of view, beliefs and assumptions, and allows you to glimpse the world through their eyes.

You can even look back at yourself in Viewpoint One and see yourself from that person's perspective.

Viewpoint Three: You now act as an observer, watching what is happening, and possibly forming opinions about the subjects of observation (Viewpoints One and Two). You are dissociated (outside your own body) from both yourself and the other person, and simply observing the interactions of these two people.

In Viewpoint Three, it's like you're a fly on the wall watching the interaction between two people.

We can often spend our lives inhabiting one viewpoint (and not necessarily Viewpoint One), which limits our understanding and therefore our ability to interact with others.

Being able to switch points of view and consider multiple perspectives gives you much greater insight of others' views of the world.

With practice, you can learn to live in Viewpoint One as your home base and move to Viewpoints Two and Three to understand more about others.

As you practise moving between these viewpoints you will become more aware of your tone of voice, your body language, and how you can adapt and become more flexible in your interactions with others.

When I run this activity in workshops, participants are asked to think about a recent conversation they had which could have gone better. Then they are asked to imagine experiencing the conversation again, this time from each viewpoint.

During the debrief, they share what they noticed. This includes things like:

- 'I wasn't aware I stood like that; I appear closed-off.'
- 'I would have a different conversation now if I could have it again.'
- 'I have a better idea of how the other person was feeling.'
- 'As an observer [Viewpoint Three] watching those two people, I felt there was a complete disconnect and misunderstanding of what was being said between them.'

Your ability to grasp how another person thinks and what their interests and capabilities are will help you understand more about that person.

Use *Activity 4.3: Considering their perspective* to guide you here.

Activity 4.3: Considering their perspective

Stand up to do this exercise.

Remember a time when you had a challenging conversation with someone.

The following instructions will help you practise mentally moving from Viewpoint One (your perspective) to Viewpoint Three (the observer) to Viewpoint Two (their perspective), and then back to Viewpoint One.

Stand right behind your chair – this is your 'home base'.
1. **Viewpoint One**. Take one step directly back from home base. From this perspective, think about that conversation. Run over it again in your mind.
   Imagine looking at the other person from your eyes. What are you seeing? How are they standing? What are you hearing with your ears, what are you saying, and what are you feeling from re-experiencing this conversation? When you have finished, move back to home base.
2. **Viewpoint Three**. Take a step back and to the right-hand side of home base. Become dissociated and uninvolved as you run over the conversation once more. Simply observe

what these two people are doing. How are they standing, gesturing, listening and seeming all round? What do you notice? When you have finished, move back to home base.

3. **Viewpoint Two**. Take a step back and to the left-hand side of home base.

Try and put yourself in the other person's shoes. What are they noticing about the person in Viewpoint One? What are they seeing, hearing and feeling about this conversation? When you have finished, move back to home base.

From these different perspectives, what extra information have you gained? What insights do you have about this experience? Has your own perception changed?

EMPOWER YOUR TEAM

Empowering your team means giving them permission to act, work with a level of autonomy, and make decisions. It means building trust, creating a safe space where all members of the team feel they can reach their full potential, and developing a shared understanding of goals and outcomes.

Empowerment cannot be handed over like a gift or a task. It is not something that happens suddenly.

It's about creating the right conditions to enable team members to feel empowered. Empowering your team is important for growing a sustainable business.

A powerful way to empower the individuals in your team is to simply ask, 'How can I help you?' This is a trust-building question, and a great way to start a coaching conversation – two key components in empowering your team.

Build trust

I once worked in a team where trust between two team members was broken. Even though it was not evident to others, it meant that we never gelled as a team. We worked well individually, but never reached high-performance levels.

The term 'high-performance teams' is used a lot in corporations to describe teams that are laser-focused on their goals, achieve superior results, and outperform similar teams.

Without trust, a team is simply a group of individuals doing their own thing. It doesn't matter how capable or talented the individuals are: a team that lacks trust will not reach its full potential.

Neuroscience research indicates that trust and distrust activate different parts of the brain. Distrust is associated with the amygdala, the area of your brain triggered by stress, and leads to cortisol production.

An atmosphere of distrust in a dysfunctional team is likely to mean that team members experience continued high cortisol levels. This impacts their ability to think and reason effectively, since cortisol shuts down activity in the pre-frontal cortex, the brain's executive functioning area.

When you feel safe and trusted by the people you interact with, oxytocin is produced, which increases social confidence and connection. More oxytocin in your system increases engagement and collaboration, and allows you and the people you are interacting with to tap into the executive functioning areas of your brains.

In this environment, team members support each other and are open and transparent. This leads to highly motivated team members who assume positive intent of others and focus on mutual success.

Trust is required in any interaction you have with others if you are to reach an effective outcome.

———————————

As the leader, focusing on building trust with your team members is essential to good performance. When you don't trust someone, the effect on the team is dramatic.

———————————

Trust comes back to the way we relate to others.

Your ability to build trust with each team member means:
- **Being reliable** (doing what you say you will do). It's hard to have confidence in a person who makes promises they don't keep. Reliability means following up on and seeing through the promises and commitments you've made. If you work with someone who has a problem with reliability, you have to say something, or the relationship will suffer!

- **Accepting others** for who they are without judging. Every-one wants to be accepted for who they are, not judged, criticised, or made to feel inferior.

   There is a power to words that can make people feel accepted or judged. It is easy to inadvertently hurt some-one by being careless with the words you use. Even using technical jargon or obscure references may cause someone to feel inferior or excluded if they're not familiar with them. Avoid jargon, obscure references and in-jokes unless you're confident that everyone in the conversation is familiar with them. Practise deep listening by checking in often to make sure people are with you (listening also for what's *not* being said).

- **Being open and transparent**. One of the best leaders I have worked with creates high trust with her teams. She has many leadership skills, including being very open. She shares pretty much everything that may impact her team, and therefore they know that there will be no surprises. Openness means being straightforward and honest – saying what is true even if it is unpleasant and not what the other person wants to hear.

   People tend to want to cooperate with you more if you level with them and give them the whole story.

Think about how reliability, acceptance and openness has enhanced or limited the trust in your team relationships.

Use *Activity 4.4: Building trust* to guide you here.

Activity 4.4: Building trust

Answer the following questions to see how well you are building trust with your team.

QUESTIONS	YES	NO
1. Do you habitually share information that is relevant to the team?		
2. Do you always do what you say you will do?		
3. Do you protect one-on-one team meeting times (meaning that they don't get bumped if 'more important' meetings come up)?		
4. Do you keep your promises or explain (are open about) why they can't be kept?		
5. Do you ask open questions to extend both your own and the team's thinking?		
6. Does each member of your team feel valued?		
7. Are you aware of the reaction of the people you are interacting with? For example, are they opening up or shutting down when you speak?		
8. Are you eliminating words that may create fear and distrust?		
9. Do you foster inclusion of all team members?		
10. Do you appreciate and acknowledge the team as a whole, as well as individuals' efforts?		
11. Do you regularly celebrate successes (of both individuals and the team)?		
12. Do you encourage team members to build on each other's capacity and capability?		

The more times you answer 'yes', the higher the trust in your team will be. You should periodically retake this questionnaire to measure your progress, with an aim to have 100% 'yes' answers over time.

Being reliable and open and accepting others are oxytocin-producing behaviours that help you build trust unconsciously. Not only does your ability to connect lead to improved performance, but your work is also more enjoyable, as you are hanging out with a group of people you like. Building trust in a team means they feel trusted, and that it's safe to explore new opportunities, take risks, and aim higher.

Oxytocin is a nurturing hormone; it's usually associated with childbirth, as it helps mothers bond with their newborn babies. However, all of us produce oxytocin when we feel safe, socially confident and trusted.

Oxytocin causes us to be less anxious, to experience rapport with others, and to feel energised. It helps us tap into our pre-frontal cortex (the executive functioning part of our brain), which is where we do our higher-order thinking.

To help others learn to build trust and increase levels of oxytocin, one of the first skills I teach my clients in both group and one-on-one sessions is how to create rapport with others.

Creating rapport

A Neuro Linguistic Programming (NLP) definition of rapport is, 'the ability to reduce difference between oneself and another at unconscious levels to promote a harmonious relationship.'

Though it's often taken for granted, rapport is a foundation for good relationships – even with people we don't like!

Building rapport quickly with someone makes them feel that we are just like them, and a level of trust will form.

When you have rapport with someone you feel safe to be curious, you listen more deeply, and trust builds between you. Being able to build rapport consciously is a technique you can learn.

Rapport is not about liking someone or agreeing with them (although it often happens naturally with people you like). It is not empathy or mimicking the other person. Rapport is a technique to build a harmonious relationship with another person, which facilitates effective communication.

You can actively and consciously build rapport with people, even when there's no previous connection or relationship. You can do this by:

- Matching their physical gestures and posture,
- Matching the tone, pace and volume of their voice,
- Matching their language,
- Matching the rhythm and pace of their breath, and
- Matching their values or emotions.

By watching a person for non-verbal cues and listening for language patterns, you can adapt your own language and behaviour to harmonise with them and establish a deep level of rapport. This is accomplished through something called 'pacing and leading'.

In 'pacing', you pick up key verbal and non-verbal cues from another person and feed them back to match their model of the world. Pacing or matching their non-verbal communication creates the sense that you are just like them. You essentially step into their shoes and communicate with them in their own way of speaking and through their own way of being.

'Leading' involves attempting to change or enrich another person's behaviour or thinking process by subtly shifting your own verbal and behavioural patterns in the desired direction, then having them follow.

You can use 'pace to lead' to test if you are in rapport. After pacing someone and matching them, try shifting your posture. For example, if you are both leaning forward in your chairs, then you lean back, and they match your movement within a minute or so, and you move again, and they follow, and so on, this is evidence that a level of rapport has been established.

When you consciously practise building rapport with others, it becomes automatic; then, communication become easier and more effective, regardless of whom you are interacting with. Do this with your team and the levels of trust will increase.

Activity 4.5: How to practise building rapport

Practise by building rapport with each person you meet, including everyone you talk to on the phone, in virtual meetings, and people whom you communicate with via email or other written correspondence.

Wherever you are, notice the people around you. Notice if groups of people are in rapport.

Body rapport
- Match posture
- Match breathing
- Match gestures
- Match eye blink rate
- Match spinal tilt

Voice rapport
- Match tone/pitch
- Match volume
- Match speed

Coach them

Daniel Goleman, in his book *The New Leaders*, talks about the six essential leadership styles, one of which is coaching. The coaching leadership style is considered to have a 'highly positive impact on culture and helps improve an individual's performance by building long-term capabilities.'

Coaching is a superpower that will help you to step back so the team can step up.

In the story at the start of this chapter, Alice didn't realise she was coaching the people queuing at her desk, as she had always thought coaching was a long sit-down meeting with someone. These by-the-desk conversations were starting to build her coaching muscle.

Seth Godin, in a blog post titled "A coaching paradox", tells us that:

> 'At the top tier of just about any sort of endeavour, you'll find that the performers have coaches.
>
> Pianists, orators and athletes all have coaches. In fact, it would be weird if we heard of someone on stage or on the field who didn't have one. And yet, in the world of business, they're seen as the exception.
>
> [...] It turns out that the people with the potential to benefit the most from a coach are often the most hesitant, precisely because of what coaching involves.
>
> Talking about our challenges. Setting goals. Acknowledging that we can get better. Eagerly seeking responsibility...'

Your ability to coach your team is what helps you bring out the best in your team.

Helping your team to work out answers for themselves is exactly what happens when you learn how to coach instead of answer.

At its simplest, coaching is your ability to ask questions, listen to the answers, and encourage the other person to come up with their own ideas and solutions.

It is the art of drawing out the knowledge or awareness of the other person by using open-ended questions to reach an outcome.

Many managers are overwhelmed with the amount of work they have, and adding one-on-one coaching conversations to their already overloaded day is not considered important. But coaching is easier than you think!

There is no need to make a coaching conversation a big deal.

These conversations can happen:
- In a formal one-on-one,
- While standing at your desk (like Alice), or
- While having a quick corridor conversation.

Developing your ability to get people to think about something from a different perspective, to consider alternatives, and come up with a solution or new idea is what you are aiming to achieve.

Depending on the sort of leader you are, you may find that people want to be spoon-fed the answers (like Alice's team used to be). These individuals need to be firmly steered towards considering what they can come up with themselves.

Many times, the people you coach are specialists whose knowledge about what they do will exceed your own.

_____

Your role is to question, listen and encourage effectively so they draw on their own knowledge and experiences to identify ways to move forward.

_____

If previously you have preferred to give the answers, it will be difficult to move from 'telling' to 'asking'.

Even though you were an expert in your old role, you don't need to be the expert in a coaching conversation. Once you believe that everyone has all the resources that they need to achieve what they want, your role in the conversation is to help bring this to their awareness.

There are good examples of coaching questions in the previous Section *Be curious and ask questions*. Other useful coaching questions are:

- What is preventing you …? (Used when someone is stuck and not sure how to proceed.)
- How will you know when you have achieved that? (What evidence will they need to know if it has been successful?)
- What does success look like?
- What's the real challenge for you with this?
- For what purpose …? (Used to define the reason for wanting to do this.)

Activity 4.6: Coaching

Coaching someone can be as informal as asking them a question when they drop by your desk, or as formal as booking a sixty-minute one-on-one meeting with them.

The more often you step into the coaching space, the stronger your coaching muscle will become.

Your questions can lead to deeper understanding for you and for them.

Looking at the following coaching questions, think about where you could use them. What sort of meetings do you have with your team where you can bring these questions into play? For instance, it could be during a one-on-one performance review, or a team meeting where you ask the whole team these questions.

Pick a couple of questions and use them the next time you're meeting with one of your team members to draw out their knowledge or ideas, or to discover where they may need specific guidance.

- What do you want to focus on during this conversation?
- What have you considered so far?
- What's the biggest challenge with this?
- What can you/we change about how it's done currently?
- What if the current assumptions were not true?
- What if the opposite were true?
- What other alternatives could work/what other alternatives could we consider?

- If we did do it this way, what does success look like?
- What is the first step?

Stretch them

When you know more about your team and understand what makes them tick, there is more opportunity to build their capability by giving them different opportunities.

Stretch assignments are projects or tasks that are not part of a person's normal role.

Try to understand where your team members are coming from and what they like to do: it will define the type of work you can give them. It also helps you to select the right person to complete a task for the right reasons.

Stretching individuals to do work that may be new to them and provide growth opportunities field-tests their skills and abilities. These temporary 'try-outs' can also allow you to solve real business issues by getting others to work out solutions you may not have considered.

Stretch assignments are the biggest career enablers in unleashing an individual's potential. In a *Harvard Business Review* article titled '21st-Century Talent Spotting', Claudio Fernández-Aráoz shared research in which 823 international executives were asked to look back at their careers. Seventy-one per cent of these senior leaders identified stretch assignments as key to their career progression.

Your team members will become more committed when they believe you, their boss, supports their ongoing growth and development.

As the workplace continues to become disrupted by change, you should have the opportunity to redefine and hone your skills – just like your team.

Some questions to consider:
- Who in your team needs further development?
- Who needs to develop the skill this project requires? (For example, development of analytical skills or interpersonal skills.)
- Who has been doing the same work over and over and needs an opportunity to try something new?

Offering stretch roles and assignments is one way for you to harness and increase your team's talents.

Provide opportunities for *all* your team, not just a select few.

_____

Remember, the person who may be able to do this task easily and fastest may not be the right person from a growth point of view.

_____

When you provide these opportunities to a member of your team, support that person to develop the right skills and succeed. How to do this will be covered in detail in chapter 5, when I focus on how you are communicating.

BE FUTURE-FOCUSED

As we wrap up this chapter, let's imagine where you're at in twelve months' time after applying some of the strategies I've described.

You have been working closely with your team, and your awareness of their capabilities and interests has grown immensely.

There is much more engagement and trust between you and the team. Capability has lifted and the culture is one of support and inclusion. You have learnt much more about each individual team member's capability.

You feel encouraged that you have space in your week. Your work hours are more reasonable, and you can focus on work you didn't have time for previously.

Your confidence is growing, and you feel you can step back, get out of the team's way, and give them the freedom to learn and try new things.

———————————

You are creating an environment in which the team is willing to experiment, fail, learn from their failures, and experiment again – you've started the engine and it's firing.

———————————

LEARN AND LEAD

A case study

Christine had been an excellent program manager for a large international bank in the United Kingdom. She was promoted to lead her team, who all operated remotely from her, with no previous leadership experience.

When Christine took over the team, she observed a lack of motivation, direction, and career and personal development plans. There was no real knowledge-sharing and very little proactivity. Team members didn't work as a cohesive unit.

She realised that her team was stuck, and she wanted to discover how to move them to high-performing.

Christine started reading about leadership and applying what she was learning. She spent time with each team member to find out more about them and what they were interested in. She took the team away for a day to focus on team-building and shared what she was learning about becoming a high-performing team.

Christine has built her leadership skills from the ground up, focusing on the team and lifting their capability.

Learning to hand over her work was hard at first. Christine had to learn to step back, because as the expert who used to do this work she had to learn to trust her team to do it.

Christine now strongly believes in the power of the individual, and as a leader she gets out of people's way to give the team freedom to flourish.

Understanding the team, coaching and empowering them, has helped Christine gently move people to a place where they're responsible for coming up with work solutions and options, and making recommendations.

They have each stepped up, owned their skills, and are flourishing in their roles as a result.

Five years on, when Christine looks at her team now, there is strong positivity, hope for the future, and belief in themselves. All team members have personal development plans which they are all progressing in, and several have had promotions.

Christine is proud to say that they have become a high-performing team, and get far greater results than other similar teams in the organisation.

Increasing awareness of others' strengths and capabilities helps you to step back, get out of your own way, and give others the freedom to flourish or fail, which is all part of learning and leading.

CHAPTER 4 SUMMARY AND ACTIONS

Start Your Engines is about getting the best out of your team. The more you know about each of your team members, the more you can determine the work that best plays to their strengths. Ultimately, this lifts them and helps the whole team thrive.

Knowing your team is about:

- Being able to listen to connect and really understand what is being said,
- Being curious and asking questions to help them explore their thinking, and
- Considering their perspective and being able to step into their shoes.

Empowering your team is about:

- Creating a relationship with each team member to build trust,
- Coaching everyone who directly reports to you to bring out their best thinking, and
- Providing stretch opportunities to help them level up.

ACTION

- Use *Activity 4.1* to identify how well you know your team and find ways to discover more about them.
- Consider how you are listening with *Activity 4.2*.

- Consider your team's perspective. Using the Perceptual Positions in *Activity 4.3*, step into the observer's shoes (Viewpoint 3), and then step into the other person's shoes (Viewpoint 2).
- Use *Activity 4.4* to identify what you are doing or not doing to build trust within your team.
- Practise building rapport with everyone and anyone. *Activity 4.5* gives tips on how and what you need to do to build rapport.
- Use *Activity 4.6* to step into the coaching space. Experiment with these questions to coach your team.

It's time to read on and find out how you can get underway.

CHAPTER 5:

GET UNDERWAY – CHANGE HOW YOU ARE COMMUNICATING

Bill is the CEO of a small organisation. When he stepped into the role, he discovered that his leadership team, many of whom had been in their roles for years, were operating at the wrong level.

They were so immersed in the day-to-day minutiae of the organisation that they couldn't get their heads up and focus on the work they should be doing at their level.

Bill's plans for the organisation were expansive, but he kept finding that he was being dragged into the details. There were staffing problems, morale issues, and lack of trust. The culture wasn't great.

Pretty much everyone in the organisation was operating at the wrong level. There was no opportunity to focus on future direction, make strategic decisions, and improve the culture.

Bill's leadership group wasn't functioning as a team. They were a group of individuals protecting their own turf and putting the needs and wants of their teams ahead of the good of the organisation. It was very much a silo-based culture.

Bill knew this organisation needed to start working together.

He started with something he considered quite small. He changed how he spoke to his direct reports about what they needed to do.

Instead of telling them about the task or project and leaving it at that, he spent more time describing what he wanted to achieve, why he wanted to achieve it, and what the result would look like. He linked each piece of work back to a bigger organisational outcome.

The degree of detail he went into depended on the capability of that team member. He also gave them a clear picture of how far their decision-making authority extended, and when they would have to come back to him for approval.

At first, Bill was a bit nervous that his reports would object to what he thought might come across as patronising. However, to his surprise, they took on the work and started doing it well.

In hindsight, Bill realised that when he first stepped into his role, he had expected a degree of professionalism and expertise from his leadership team that wasn't there.

This was a group of people who had been entrenched in this conservative organisation for years, under a previous CEO who had been in their role for over twenty years.

They hadn't been challenged and hadn't experienced any sort of growth or changes in their thinking for a long time.

The managers had been encouraged to focus downwards on their team without looking up and out to see the impact on the broader organisation.

By subtly changing how he communicated to this group, Bill saw that, over time, they started to move out of the doing and into the leadership space. They started to listen to each other and work together in a more collegial manner.

This meant Bill could also start to level up and focus on moving the organisation forward.

Levelling up your team is about leverage – working with your team to amplify yours and the team's results.

_____

When everyone levels up, there is a
collective up-lift for the organisation.

_____

ARE YOU A DELIBERATE DELEGATOR?

It's now time to bring everything together to tap into your potential, as well as that of your team. Like Bill discovered, it is the small changes that have the biggest impact.

As you have worked your way through this book, you have learnt how to:

- Clear the Decks – by completing a Task and Mindset Audit
- Start Your Engines – by gaining more knowledge about each member of your team and how to empower them to step up

You are now at a place where you can focus on your role and create some space and balance in your life.

———————————

The key to doing this well is to become a Deliberate Delegator.

———————————

If you used to be a control freak, doing all the work yourself instead of allowing your team to do it, you were held back from focusing on the work appropriate for your level of seniority.

The question to ask yourself is, 'What sort of leader are you currently?' Are you a:

- Doer,
- Persuader,
- Supporter, or
- Influencer?

And where do you want to be?

Figure 5.1 identifies whether you are focusing on high-value or low-value tasks, and with a present or future focus.

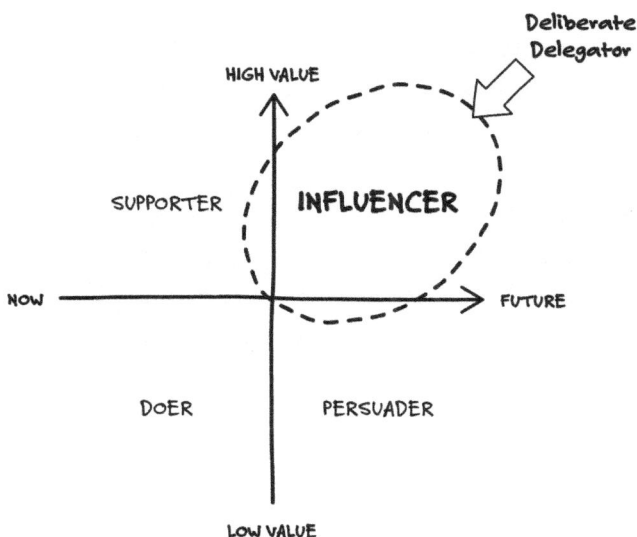

Figure 5.1: The levels of thinking model

The Doer

If you're a Doer, your attention is still focused on the tasks you are working on, and you are not aware of what your team is doing. You are immersed in the details, holding on to work you used to do and still probably enjoy, and have a range of reasons why you can't hand it over.

At this level, you're overwhelmed and drowning in being too busy and doing too much. You are in the moment and reacting to everything. You expect the team to get on with their work, but that may not have been made clear to them. They are not sure what they should be doing, as you don't have time to show or explain it to them.

You find it hard to let go and continue to work on tasks that are below your pay grade.

This lower-level work should be done by your team. When you're busy doing, your team will struggle to tap into your expertise, and they will be pushed down to a lower level of detail.

The Persuader

As a Persuader, you trust your team to some extent and hand over some tasks. While you have a future vision for what you want the team to achieve, it is low-level work and not strategic.

You are task-focused without considering what you should be working on or how everything fits together. You are kept busy persuading and advising the team on minutiae rather than the big picture, and you may miss opportunities that a more strategic mindset would see.

You are doing a lot of work that is not urgent and should be delegated to your team. You need to move from doing these lower-level tasks and start to focus on the work relevant to your pay grade.

The Supporter

As a Supporter, you can pass work on knowing that your team can do it. You are focusing on high-value work, but you are being reactive rather than proactive, and are focused on the present moment without considering future impacts.

There is no strategic visioning or planning. This is okay for the short term; however, spending too long here supporting your team means that there is no opportunity to look at the future direction. As a team, you start 'spinning your wheels' and not really getting anywhere.

You need to be able to level up and get a view of how this work plays out for future gains.

The Influencer

If your leadership style is Influencer, you are on the way to being a Transformational Leader and creating a dynamic culture. You and your team are heading in the same direction. The team is performing well and you can focus on high-value, future-oriented, strategic work.

This means you're stepping up, thinking more strategically, and focusing on what you need to do as a team to achieve outcomes.

You are focusing on the work appropriate for your level of seniority, and are able to look up and out to see how everything fits together. You are influencing the direction for the team, and considering what future success looks like.

As an Influencer, you will inspire your team and lift them to higher levels of operation.

At this level, you:
- Understand what your role is and what it isn't,
- Know that what you used to do, liked to do, and were good at may not be part of your role now,
- Know that you are not the only one capable of completing a task or piece of work, and
- Invest time in developing your team so you can free up

time to work on other, more important projects appropriate for your role.

Instead of saying, 'I don't have time to train someone,' you understand this is an investment of your time that will pay off for you tenfold.

Working as an Influencer allows you to create space. You can comfortably take time off and know that your team will operate well when you're away.

Becoming a Deliberate Delegator

In *Figure 5.1* above, you may have noticed the bubble encompassing the Influencer space titled 'Deliberate Delegator'. You cannot be an Influencer unless you can effectively delegate.

The work you have done as you have progressed through this book has laid the foundation to enable you to delegate well.

Being prepared to hand work over and let others do it will start to free up space in your day.

Instead of working ten to twelve (or more) hours per day, plus weekends, you will get time back and be able to put some balance into your life.

As you build this delegator muscle, you can start to structure your day and begin working on the priorities appropriate for your role.

A great test for you and your team is to see what happens if you take expected or even unexpected leave. How does the team cope?

_____

Do projects falter or proceed in your absence?

_____

When you first begin to delegate, there are a couple of strategies that may trip you up and limit the effectiveness of what you want to achieve.

The Buy-Back. This is when you end up doing a task you thought you had delegated.
You say things like:
- 'I'll check with...' Involving someone else means that the person you have delegated to can't do anything until you have.
- 'Let me think about it...' This takes the onus off the person to think any further about the task.
- 'Leave it, I'll...' Completely taking it back and out of their hands, you end up doing it yourself.

This means the delegation fails. The work remains with you because there is no progress until you do something.

Put in Limbo. This is where you halt progress.
You say things like:
- 'Send me something on it...' Which means that person must draft up a plan, send it to you, and then wait for your response.

- 'Why don't you check with…' When you tell someone to check with someone else, this not only slows down progress but can also mean that they get mixed messages from that other person.
- 'See me later about…' Which tells them that they can't really do much until they have checked with you later.
- 'We'll have to do something…' Which blurs the lines of responsibility – do they go ahead and 'do something', or are they waiting for you to 'do something'?

You are pausing any progress towards getting this work done.

If work is paused or halted, or if you have taken it back, then you are frustrating that team member because there is no clear direction. Setting each person up for success to do their role well, and giving them the confidence to take on more and different work, is crucial.

Delegating is, at its simplest, about trust. Yet that is not so simple. If trust is in place in your team, you will feel comfortable delegating. If that trust isn't in place, or you don't have enough evidence of your team's capability, the 'Buy-Back' and 'Put in Limbo' scenarios come into play.

Or, you can turn into a control freak and micromanage your team members.

Knowing someone's level of capability is a tricky thing. The person may be capable, but you don't yet have evidence of it. Understanding your assurance strategy is crucial: this is what you need to hear and see to believe that this person can do the job.

Without this, you may not get the feeling that this person can do the work to your satisfaction. If the assurance strategy isn't in place, then you start looking over their shoulder, checking on what they are doing, contacting them daily, and so on. As a result, you turn into that control freak. And that's something you want to avoid.

Avoiding becoming a control freak means changing how you communicate with team members and how they communicate with you.

When you use delegation the right way:
- Productivity increases,
- Team engagement and collaboration increases, and
- The team can take on extra responsibility.

Of course, there are parts of your role that you should never delegate.

Things like:
- Performance feedback for people reporting directly to you,
- Disciplinary actions,
- Politically sensitive tasks, and
- Confrontations arising from interpersonal conflict between team members.

Clearing the Decks and Starting Your Engines have set the scene. The final step in moving on from being a control freak is dependent on how well you communicate to each of your team members.

———————————

Giving clear instructions for the work you are asking someone to do is critical to the successful completion of that work.

———————————

8 INGREDIENTS FOR CLEAR INSTRUCTIONS

The dilemma about delegating anything is that when you did the work you used to do in your former role, you probably did it effortlessly, quickly, and with a bit of pizzazz.

This same work may not be done as well or as fast by someone doing the task for the first or second time.

This means staying open to what you may perceive as imperfection.

———————————

How you delegate is as important as what you delegate.

———————————

When you ask someone to take on an extra piece of work, building their confidence in doing this means saying things like:
- 'You've got this – I know you can do it.'
- 'I've given this to you because you have all the necessary skills to do it well.'

- 'Your persistence in finding and engaging the right people makes you the right person for this project.'
- 'I'm confident in your ability to do this.'

Giving someone extra work also shows your confidence in their ability. It makes them step up and take more responsibility for its completion.

Their ownership of this work means the project is more likely to get done without you having to intervene.

The level of detail you provide will vary depending on the capability of the person you delegate to. You will have a much better understanding of this from building your awareness of the team.

In terms of delegating, think about each person's capability to take on what you want to delegate and rate them on a scale from one to ten.

- At the low end is one to four out of ten. This is someone with very little experience or skills. They may be new to the team, new to this type of work, or will need more help to complete this work.

  Giving someone with very low capability a task may cause you more work, as you will have to watch everything they are doing. In this case, it may be more useful to have them shadow you or someone with experience in doing the task to learn how to do it.

- For people with moderate capability (the five-to-seven range), you can delegate tasks readily. How much autonomy you can give them to operate without your involvement will depend on what the work is.

This person needs regular check-ins to see how they're going, and if they need any support. If you've given them a high-level task, you may want to take a more hands-on approach.

- Someone who you rate as an eight to ten out of ten is likely to be very familiar with this work, and maybe even better at executing it than you. They won't need much guidance, if any, and won't appreciate being told too much or have you checking on them too often. Otherwise, it might make them feel like they're being micromanaged.

In each case, the *8 Ingredients for clear instructions*, as shown in *Figure 5.2*, will change how you communicate to ensure the right level of support and instruction is provided regardless of the capability of the person.

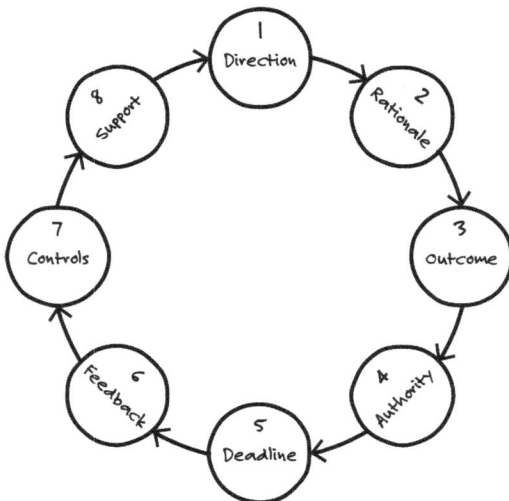

Figure 5.2: 8 Ingredients for clear instructions

1. Directions

The first step in delegating effectively is providing clear directions. Ask yourself:

- Do you clearly understand what this task is, and have you explained it clearly?
- Have you checked in to be sure your team member understands what it is you have asked them to do?

We may feel we have explained something well, yet the meaning of what we have said is dependent on what the other person understands.

This means there is always a degree of misunderstanding or misinterpretation to what people think we are saying.

In *Deep Listening*, Oscar Trimboli talks about the 125/400-word rule, which identifies the gap between what we can say and what we can process. We can speak at about 125-175 words a minute, yet we listen and process at 400 words a minute.

For any given thought or instruction that you want to express verbally, you need to understand that you will probably only get out a fraction of what you are thinking in spoken words.

This also means that the listener is adding their own thinking to what you are saying, and therefore making their own meaning.

Making sure that people understand the meaning you are making, and that you understand their meaning, helps to provide clear directions.

By 'double-clicking' on the meaning of words used in conversations, you create a shared understanding. 'Double-clicking' was a reference originally used for 'pressing a computer mouse twice' to open a folder or document.

Judith E. Glaser, in her book *Conversational Intelligence*, used this term to describe a technique that can help people understand and communicate better, and enable them to activate and explore valuable insights, memories and wisdom that are made available through conversations.

Double-clicking is a way to expand on the words we hear. Remember I said that we can speak at about 125-175 words a minute, yet we listen and process at 400 words a minute. Often, those extra words we add to process what someone is saying is not what they mean at all.

Double-clicking allows us to open up and create more understanding about the words they are saying.

For example, if someone says they want the team to have a successful year, double-clicking on the word 'success' helps us understand what they mean. Otherwise, we might interpret success to mean 'leaving on time every day'. For them, success might mean 'reaching our profit figures'.

Unless we ask and double-click on their words, we are potentially at risk of a massive misunderstanding.

This is more than simply asking, 'Do you understand?' Because, at a surface level, they do understand, so they will likely say, 'Yes.' If you delve a little deeper (double-click) and ask them to tell you *what* they understand, you can then check if that matches what you meant.

2. Rationale

Have you ever completed work that ended up not being used, or turned out not to be needed, making you feel that you had wasted hours of your time?

Imagine this happening to someone you delegated a task to. They spent hours working to complete what you asked, only to find that there was no real reason for doing it. It wasn't needed after all.

If you don't understand why this work needs to be done, then it isn't ready to delegate.

Before delegating a task, ask yourself: do you understand the reason for completing this task, project, or major piece of work?

―――――――――――――

As the leader, before delegating something, determine and then advise the person who will be doing it the reason why this piece of work is required.

―――――――――――――

A simple exercise is to dig a little deeper into why you want this piece of work done. Spend some time to develop an understanding of 'why'.

Here's an example of how to do that. Ask 'for what purpose…?' -type questions:

- **Question**: 'For what purpose do you want this piece of work completed?'
- **Answer**: 'So that our team has the necessary tools to track our KPIs.'
- **Question**: 'For what purpose do you want tools to track your KPIs?'
- **Answer**: 'So that our team can become self-sufficient in their work.'
- **Question**: 'For what purpose do you want the team to be self-sufficient in their work?'
- **Answer**: 'So that they can determine the work required to meet and even exceed our targets.'
- **Question**: 'For what purpose do you want them to determine their own work?'
- **Answer**: 'So that they feel they are fully contributing, feel valued, and are using their expertise so the whole team can succeed.'

In this example, you want the piece of work completed to allow individuals in the team to feel they are valued and contributing their expertise to ensure the whole team succeeds.

Doing this exercise before you delegate something means you have a deep understanding of why this work needs to be completed. Stating this to the person you are delegating to means more buy-in from them.

3. Outcome

Imagine you have arrived at an airport (let's say Melbourne Airport), got into a taxi or Uber, and said, 'I don't want to go to Essendon, or Dandenong, or Malvern.'

Where does the driver take you? Nowhere or anywhere! Both will work if neither of you know where to go.

When you delegate, knowing the outcome of the task or project you are assigning to someone else is crucial.

If you don't have that knowledge, neither you nor the person you are delegating to will know where this piece of work is going or when it is complete.

Isn't it frustrating when you delegate work to others and you don't get the results you're after, or you must redo work that you delegated because it wasn't done properly?

Make sure you understand the outcome you expect when this piece of work is completed. If you understand it, then you can communicate it.

Please note, this isn't about telling the person *how* something needs to be achieved. Leave that up to them. This is about *what* it looks like upon completion.

Making sure the outcomes are clearly communicated increases the likelihood that the task/project will be completed effectively.

For example, I may want to delegate the preparation of a board paper. If I simply say, 'Please prepare the next board paper,' then I'm likely going to have to rework the result.

If I say, 'Please prepare a board paper that provides information about our proposed new projects so that the board can make an informed decision to proceed,' then I have clearly communicated that the intended outcome is to get board approval for our new projects.

This allows the person to whom I have delegated the task to do the necessary work to achieve this outcome.

4. Authority
Have you ever worked for someone who is so protective of their turf that they won't allow you to speak to anyone more senior than they are? Do they get nervous if their boss wants to talk to you, which means you can't do your job properly as you are unable to get the information from the right people?

Oh – and there is a huge trust issue!

Maybe this is you, if you're someone who can't let go of control and needs to be across everything.

On the flip side, have you ever experienced the frustration of delegating a piece of work to a team member, only to have them check in with you several times a day to ask, 'Can you contact this person?' or, 'Can you approve this expenditure?' and so on.

When you provide the necessary and appropriate level of authority, your team feels more empowered, trusted and engaged.

Effective delegation moves authority downwards throughout the team, and supports the team members' development towards becoming the future leaders they may aspire to be. This creates a culture that is renewing and regenerating.

Suddenly, you are leading at the right level and the team is teaming at the right level. Everyone has levelled up.

This allows the team to face issues without fear and allows individuals to speak up. They listen to others' perspectives, and stick up for their own rights and the rights of others. They feel safe to talk about problems they may be experiencing.

Level of authority refers to the furthest extent of autonomy that a team member can exercise before they must check in with you or others for approval.

What level of authority does this person have, or need, to complete this piece of work?

Does this person know:

- Who they can contact for further information, support or resources?
- What budget they must complete this work under?
- What decisions they can make?
- What information they can send out to the team and broader organisation about this work, or if they can send any information at all?

Define the range of decision-making and responsibility the person has to do this work before they must seek out further approval from you.

5. Deadline

Have you ever been handed some work to complete with no clear indication when it is due?

I don't know if you're like me, but if someone gives me something to do without a deadline, this leads to heaps of procrastination because I keep delaying getting started on it.

If you don't provide a deadline when you delegate you'll become frustrated, as will the person doing the work, because there may be no sign of completion.

Imagine you've delegated something and haven't provided a deadline. This will cause your team member to procrastinate. How important can it be, they think, as you haven't said when you need it?

Then you forget that you handed it over, and weeks later realise that the work hasn't been done. And all hell breaks loose.

Who's at fault? Both of you. You for not saying when the work is due and for not checking in, and them for not asking you when you wanted it completed by.

This used to be me. I would hand over a piece of work to a team member, and be in such a hurry that I'd give them just the high-level information and then forget to tell them when I wanted it back. *Every* time I did this, I was disappointed with the result.

When you delegate to someone, giving that person the deadline to complete the work is essential. Otherwise, they are likely to let other work get ahead of it.

———————

Time is not the issue: delegation works in any timeframe if it is communicated clearly.

———————

Be real about the deadline: don't make up a time when the work is due and then not do anything with the work for weeks (if at all). This is completely demoralising to the person when they see their hard work get ignored (I know – it has happened to me plenty of times in the past).

Setting deadlines is key to focusing on the important parts of your role and creating competence and confidence in your team members.

6. Feedback

This means both giving feedback to the person doing the work, and getting feedback from them about their understanding of what you have asked them to do.

If it's a large piece of work requiring controls and follow-up (see number 7 below), feedback should be regular and ongoing.

———————————

Feedback reduces or eliminates confusion, creates clarity, and motivates the person to do a good job.

———————————

First up, get feedback from your team member about what they understand about this work. Do they understand what you want them to do?

Then, it's crucial that they understand your assurance strategy.

What do you need to hear and see to know that this person understands what it is you want them to do? If you're in the trust-building phase with this person and they simply say, 'Yes, got it,' and move on, this may not be enough to give you assurance of their understanding.

Maybe you want to hear them describe exactly what it is that they will be doing so you can understand their thinking and reasoning processes. You may also want to know more about what they are going to do and how it's going to be done.

As this work continues, feedback is ongoing and is a two-way process. You need to let people know what you need from them to feel assured about how things are progressing. They need to hear from you about things that may help or hinder them, and how they have performed so far.

Match your feedback to your team member's level of capability. Someone new to a task and learning as they go will need more detailed and specific feedback. Highly capable people require feedback as well to tell them how they're going or if there is something they need to do differently.

Think of a time that you were asked to complete a piece of work, were happy with it when you did so, yet days and weeks went by without your boss acknowledging what you had done.

What about those times when you've delegated work to others, and you were disappointed with the result? Did you swallow your comments and just redo it in the way you wanted in the first place?

Delegation, thoughtfully considered, requires us to keep a stream of feedback going with the person we are delegating to.

If you aren't aware of the need for ongoing feedback:
- You may find yourself continually redoing work that you had delegated,
- You won't know how much of the work has been done, and
- The person you have delegated to may start doing something completely different from what you had requested.

Feedback doesn't mean nit-picking every small detail or hovering over the person's shoulder and saying, '*No* – do it this way.'

---

*A confused mind leads to confused outcomes,
and feedback counteracts this.*

On completion of this work, remember to thank your team member and recognise their efforts.

Mediocre leaders manage time, great managers lead their teams. Use the gold in your team – delegating effectively finds it.

7. Controls/follow-up

What milestones have you jointly agreed upon to track, review and communicate progress?

Think about a time in the past when you've delegated a piece of work, only to check in weeks later to find it was a disaster.

If you find yourself continually bringing projects back onto track after they have lost their way, then you may not have adequately covered this step.

If you are familiar with project management, this will be a doddle for you. If you aren't, then it's important to understand that stage gates or milestones are necessary for work that takes two weeks or more.

_____

When you delegate something, ask the person doing the work to estimate the key stages of the task, and then determine what they can report on and when to indicate whether the work is on time, on budget, and within scope.

_____

Make sure they have documented these and set up times with you to go through each stage and its progress.

Controls or follow-up for a smaller task (less than a couple of weeks) could simply be saying something like, 'Check in with me each Wednesday and let me know how you're going.'

When controls are put in place it helps the team member to stay on track, provides you with assurance about the project status, and allows you to support your team member if things are heading off track.

It means 'no surprises' when done well.

8. Support
Lastly, let the team member know support is available for them to ensure completion of this work.

Have you ever assumed that someone knows how to do the thing you've asked them to do, and then days later you discover they are totally out of their depth and that piece of work hasn't gone anywhere?

Or, have you checked in and realised that this person does not have the skills you had assumed, which ends up blowing out the time and cost to complete the work?

Providing adequate support allows a team member to have the confidence to get on with it.

Support can come in many forms. It could be:
- Training and development to build specific skills
- Coaching a team member or finding someone to mentor them
- Giving them a list of people to contact who will be able to help them

It's also important to maintain your support throughout the duration of a project or assignment.

———————————————

Without the necessary support, the work
or project can go off on a tangent.

———————————————

This means you may need to step in to bring work back on track, which takes time and effort.

I had a client who realised that she hadn't provided enough support for a new team member. She had delegated a piece of work to this individual and assumed they had the required knowledge, so didn't ask if they knew how to do this work and understood what needed to be done.

Being new, this person was too afraid to say anything.

When my client checked in after a few days, that new team member was almost in tears and hadn't made a start on the work.

Understanding her mistake immediately, my client realised she should have set up the appropriate levels of support.

Now, as a result, my client checks with everyone at the beginning of each assignment and makes sure the necessary support is in place.

When support is in place, your team will stay on track and know they can check in with you at any time.

Communicate to collaborate

When you practise each ingredient described here, the way you communicate will change. You'll find that what you are saying and how it is interpreted by others will start to change.

Your listening will change, and you will start to hear things that people are saying differently. You will experience more curiosity about how people are going about doing the work, rather than feeling anxious that it's not being done as you would do it.

The confidence you have in your team and each individual member will change as your understanding of each of them grows. Your awareness of what each of them can contribute and their individual strengths and abilities will grow.

As these benefits accumulate, your team will become engaged, collaborate with you and each other more, and become better in overall team performance.

By putting these steps into practice, you become a Deliberate Delegator. There are spaces appearing in your day. There are some days when you are not running to (or logging onto) back-to-back meetings.

The queue of people at your desk (or leaving voicemails, sending emails or messages) to ask questions has disappeared.

The capability of your team has increased. Even those previously unmotivated team members are engaged in the work that you have delegated to them.

Delegating allows you to level up and start taking on the components of your role that you haven't had time to get to. It means the overwhelm you were experiencing has started to diminish.

Organisations that have a delegation culture thrive, innovate, grow and prosper – isn't that what we all want?

Activity 5.1: Team capability

Using the Task Audit checklist you completed in chapter 3, trans-fer the tasks you have identified that can be delegated. Identify who is the best person in the team to give this work to. Consider this in terms of their capability, stretch opportunities, and whether this fits with their desired career progression.

Rate their capability on a scale from 1 to 10 so you remain aware of the level of support they will need.

1. **Low capability** (1-4) means they will need more help to complete this work.
2. **Moderate capability** (5-7) means you can begin to give them some autonomy to complete this work.
3. **High capability** (8-10) means you can hand over the work and let them work it out.

TASKS	DELEGATE TO	LEVEL OF SUPPORT

Activity 5.2: 8 Ingredients for clear instructions checklist

Regardless of the level of support required, remember to use the *8 ingredients for clear instructions* to make sure you have clearly communicated what this work is. Use the following checklist to tick the components you need for clear communication.

INGREDIENTS	DESCRIPTION	YES/NO
1. DIRECTION	Have you explained the task carefully?	
2. RATIONALE	Does the team member know the reason for completing the task?	
3. OUTCOMES	Does the team member know what outcomes you expect?	
4. AUTHORITY	Has the range of decision-making and responsibility allowed without approvals been defined?	
5. DEADLINE	Does the team member know when the task has to be completed by?	
6. FEEDBACK	Have you checked that the team member understands what needs to be done and by when?	
7. CONTROLS/ FOLLOW-UP	Have you and the team member agreed on what milestones should be used to track, review and communicate progress?	
8. SUPPORT	Have you explained the support available to them to ensure completion of this task?	

GOING FROM ZERO TO TEN IN DELEGATION ABILITY

A case study
After being promoted, Donna, a senior leader from a leading global beauty brand, struggled to adjust to her new role. She was facing a big restructure, and a new challenge to coordinate a larger team. Specifically, her issues were: personal overwhelm, perceived control, not enough time, and the low sales performance of individuals and the team.

Working longer hours with an increased workload and doing more of others' work (so it would be done properly) only deepened Donna's sense of overwhelm.

Together, we identified a need to build deliberate delegation skills and move the team from focusing on individual needs to collective needs. It was also necessary to increase the effectiveness and accountability of the team to better meet and exceed organisational expectations.

Upon completion of a seven-month coaching program:
- Donna's delegation skills improved from zero out of ten at the outset to ten out of ten, and she now feels she is an expert in this area.
- Her team-development skills increased from five out of ten to nine out of ten.
- She no longer feels compelled to do the work herself and has evolved into a supportive leader with a coaching style to support each team member. Even a 'difficult' team

member has embraced this new way of operating and is now much more engaged at work.

Organisational-wide engagement surveys now show:

- The team is happier, feels more empowered, is making far fewer errors, and is doing more overall to be effective than prior to the coaching program.
- The cohesion, collaboration and effectiveness of the team has improved, in turn creating a high-performing culture.
- Pleasingly, team sales results have turned around and been called 'phenomenal'. The team achieved close to the organisation's pre-COVID-19 targets, which was completely unexpected.

CHAPTER 5 SUMMARY AND ACTIONS

Getting underway is about taking action and becoming a Deliberate Delegator. *The levels of thinking model* in *Figure 5.1* identifies whether you are an Influencer focusing on high-value, future-focused work, or if you are stuck in the Doer role focusing on low-value, in-the-moment work.

There are strategies you may be using that will trip you up and halt progress, like the Buy-Back and Put in Limbo.

Understanding each team member's capability (low, medium, high) to do the work you want to delegate is crucial to delegating effectively because the level of support for each will vary.

The *8 Ingredients for clear instructions* list in *Figure 5.2* is the roadmap to change how you are communicating and how to become a Deliberate Delegator.

ACTION

- Refer to your Task Audit checklist in chapter 3. Use *Activity 5.1: Team capability* for each task that you have identified to be delegated. Who will you delegate it to and what level of support do they need?
- Keep *Activity 5.2: 8 Ingredients for clear Instructions checklist* handy to refer to when you're delegating.

It's time to read on and transform what you are doing so you can level up in your role.

CONCLUSION:

TRANSFORM NOW

Life is too short to be stuck in a job you don't like.

After reading this book, you now know some more: about yourself and your team; about the difference between being an ineffective and a Transformational Leader; and about the need to change how you are communicating.

You have also read about how you can take back some control in your life and reduce your feeling of overwhelm.

You can tap into the brilliance of your team and have the tools to move them from a place of friction to a feeling of flow.

You have ways to connect with your team, build trust, and have better conversations, so you can now watch them grow, thrive, and step up into their roles.

So where to now?

- Go back through the exercises in this book and focus on what you can get off your plate.

- Do a Task Audit and note down everything that is taking up space in your brain, creating worry and stress. You will be surprised by how much on this list may never need to be done, or how much you can be delegating to someone else.

- Let go of the need for perfectionism – sometimes things don't need to be done to your exact standards.

- Do a Mindset Audit – what is really going on that is preventing you from levelling up? Is it fear, limiting beliefs, or overwhelm?

- Get to know your team, step into their shoes. What are they good at, what do they like to do, and how can you help them achieve that?

- Then, build more connection with the team and start to delegate effectively. Be deliberate about how you hand over tasks. Make sure to follow the *8 Ingredients for clear instructions* so you are clear about what you want done.

You can do this.
Keep focusing on developing your behavioural skills.
Learning to lead is a lifelong process.

I've worked with leaders and watched them go from a zero out of ten in managing and leading to a ten out of ten. This is inspiring. They now love what they do, and their team loves working together. Watching their overwhelm diminish and their thinking change is liberating.

As a ten out of ten, you are a Transformational LEADER.

You:
• Understand what you should be doing and what the team should be doing.
• Can let go of the technical work and let your team get on with it.
• Understand that there are different ways to achieve a result.
• Empower the team.
• Focus on meaningful, well-defined goals and outcomes that align with organisational purpose and strategy.
• Focus on the work you should be paying attention to and is appropriate for your level of seniority while doing less of the work that your team should be doing.
• Build your team's capability so they start to perform better and, over time, take on more responsibility appropriate for their level.
• Are in flow because leading is becoming effortless.
• Look up and out, and strategically focus on the future for your team.

So, go forth and focus on those behaviours you need to develop to level up and lead at the level appropriate for your pay grade – and achieve success.

Work With Me

Thanks for reading *Level Up*.

My belief is that everyone wants to do a good job. I also believe that you already have all the skills and resources needed to achieve what it is you want to achieve.

My job is to draw this out and help you tap into your expertise.

I despair at the untapped potential in organisations where people are put into boxes called a 'job description' and are not allowed to expand or grow to their full capability.

It is your role as a leader to:
- Lead at the right level,
- Develop the behavioural skills to become a leader, not a Doer, and
- Support and guide your team to reach their potential.

I'm based in a sunny beachside suburb in Melbourne, Australia. When I'm not walking along the beach with my two beautiful dogs (miniature fox terriers), I'm running virtual workshops and coaching sessions from my office.

When allowed, I also love to be at the front of a training room working with leaders like you and your teams to help lift you to brilliance, or at least help you access some of your untapped potential.

I'd love to hear how you are levelling up. Send me a message at maree@mareeburgess.com and let me know how you're going.

Sign up to my newsletter at www.mareeburgess.com/newsletter and simply reach out to book me for:

- A leadership coaching program that will fast-track your success, or
- A training program for you and your team (a series of workshops and coaching) to level up.

I'd love to work with you.

Acknowledgements

Who would have thought I'd write one book, let alone three!

Huge thanks to Donna McGeorge for encouraging me to turn my eBook about delegation into a much broader resource to help leaders lead well.

It started before that, at dinner with Donna, Tracey Ezard, and Lynne Cazaly. We were away for a girls' working (really!) retreat (pre-COVID), and they all looked at me and said, 'You know what, you are all about delegation.' It turns out they were right. Except now it is much more than that.

Thanks girls, for sending me on this delightful journey over the last couple of years. You have been there at every bump and celebration point cheering me along. I appreciate you and thank you for your continued support.

Kelly Irving – you are amazing. Thank you for working with me over the past twelve months. Thank you for telling me that I was mixing my messages and my target audience. You have turned something that was admittedly a bit rambly and all over the place into something that I think is clear, succinct and practical.

Thank you Grammar Factory: Scott MacMillan, Olivia Joerges, Carolyn Jackson, and Ania Ziemirska. I was looking for that level up (see what I did there?) in terms of the look and feel of this book as well as an enhanced level of professionalism, and you have certainly delivered.

I'm going to say a quiet thanks to my son Callon. I'm giving advance warning that I will be popping into his bookshop and rearranging the shelves so that *Level Up* is front and centre.

And thanks to my son Rhys, who had to put up with me distractedly talking with him while I finished the book.

Thank you, Tony, for always going above and beyond in taking care of me. I am grateful to have you in my life.

Lastly, for my mum, Elsie, who celebrated her 90th birthday in style earlier this year. Soon after, she left us due to a very sudden illness. You have been my guiding light throughout my life, and I miss you every day.

www.ingramcontent.com/pod-product-compliance
Lightning Source LLC
Chambersburg PA
CBHW030517210326
41597CB00013B/944